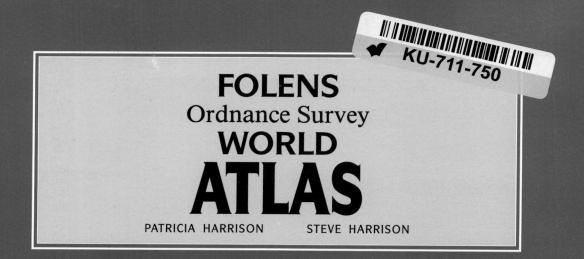

FOLENS
Ordnance Survey
WORLD
ATLAS

PATRICIA HARRISON   STEVE HARRISON

CONTENTS

ACKNOWLEDGEMENTS

The authors and publishers would like to thank the following for permission to reproduce photographs and other materials:

The Ancient Art & Architecture Collection (25; 27; 32)
Aspect Picture Library Limited (58)
Barnabys Picture Library (55)
Bossu/Sygma (40)
Bruce Coleman Limited (33)
Cleveland County Archaeology Section (10)
The Department of Transport (17)
The Environmental Picture Library (41)
Ford Motor Company Limited (21)
Greater Manchester Metro Limited (17)
The Hutchison Library (50; 51)
The National Portrait Gallery (30)
Picturepoint Limited (56; 57; 58)
Popperfoto Limited (45)
Rex Features Limited (17; 23)
The Robert Harding Picture Library (34; 54)
South American Pictures (52)
Spectrum Colour Library (34; 39; 43; 47; 59)
the Still Moving picture company (12)
Still Pictures (49)
Susan Griggs Agency (12; 21; 44; 49)
tapol: The Indonesian Human Rights Campaign (44)
Tony Stone Photolibrary – London (9; 14; 17; 19; 23; 33; 39; 41; 43; 44; 48; 50; 51; 53; 55; 56; 57; 59; 60; 61)
Tropix Photographic Library (47)
USSR PhotoLibrary (43)
The Wales Tourist Board (21)
Wildlife Matters Photographic Library (52)
ZEFA (14; 17; 33; 39; 48; 53)

The publishers have made every effort to contact copyright holders but this has not always been possible. If any have been overlooked we will be pleased to make any necessary arrangements.

To the best of the publishers' knowledge, information in this atlas was correct at the time of going to press. No responsibility can be accepted for any errors.

On pages 11, 12, 13, 14, 15, 16, 18, 20, 22, 26, 27, 28 and 30 of this atlas, mapping of Ireland is based on the Ordnance Survey with the permission of:
1) The Government of the Republic of Ireland (Permit No 5541)
2) The Controller of H.M. Stationery Office (Permit No 460)
Crown copyright reserved.

Graphics & design: Jillian Luff of Bitmap Graphics.
Artwork: Ann Baum & Peter Dennis of Linda Rogers Associates; Peter Utton of Graham-Cameron Illustration.
Cover design: Hybert Design & Type.

First published 1992 by Folens Limited, Dunstable and Dublin, and Ordnance Survey, Southampton.

© Crown Copyright 1992.

© 1992 Folens Limited, on behalf of the authors.
Folens Limited, Albert House, Apex Business Centre, Boscombe Road, Dunstable, LU5 4RL, England.

	non-net	**net**
ISBN	1 852 76330 2 (Folens)	1 852 76491 0 (Folens)
ISBN	0 319 00338 8 (OS)	0 319 00298 5 (OS)

Printed by Bath Press Colourbooks.

What is a map?

Maps have been used since prehistoric times. They help us understand the world around us.

map is a way of passing information.

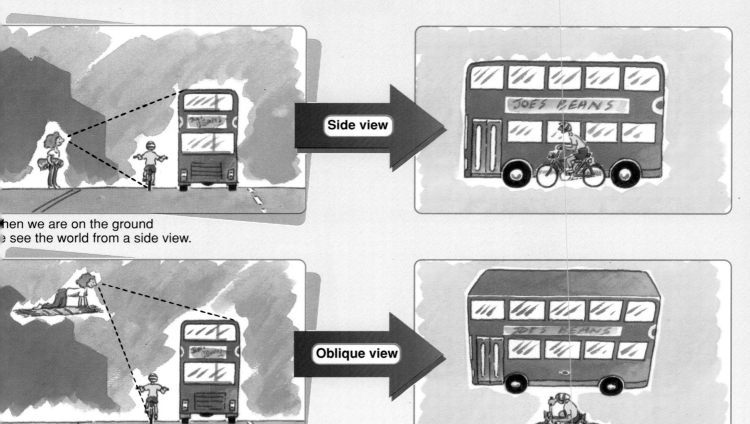

Side view

hen we are on the ground e see the world from a side view.

Oblique view

we fly on a magic carpet the world oks different. This is an oblique view.

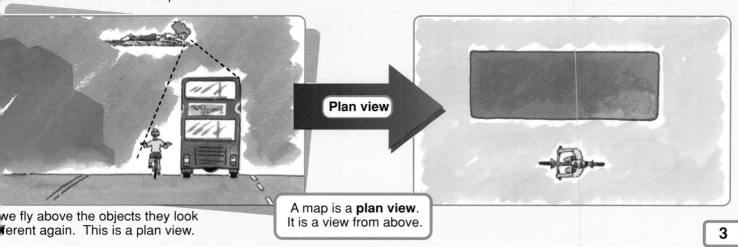

Plan view

we fly above the objects they look ferent again. This is a plan view.

A map is a **plan view**. It is a view from above.

3

Scale

The higher you are, the more area you can see.

sees

sees

sees

The lower you are, the more detail you can see.

Different maps show different amounts of deta[il]
We use the word **scale** to describe thi[s]

A builder needs a **large scale map** which shows the detail of roads, pavements and buildings.

A lorry driver needs
much **smaller scale ma[p]**
which gives informatio[n]
about main road[s]
between town[s]

This map would be no use to the lorry driver.

This map would be no use to the builder.

Choosing the right scale of map is important.

Example:
1 cm on the map stands for 1250 cm on the ground.

0   25 m

Scale 1:1250

Maps show the scale in a scale box.

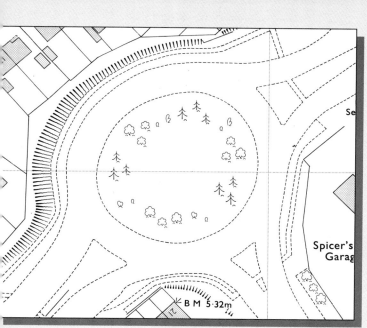

Symbols and keys

When using a large scale map we often know what is shown by its shape. Features such as traffic roundabouts, churches, running tracks and docks are easy to recognise from their shape.

Other features are not so easy to recognise. Many buildings have the same shape. In order to show which building is a post office and which is a public house, the map maker uses letter symbols.

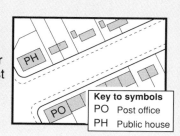

Key to symbols
PO   Post office
PH   Public house

Some maps have word, letter and picture symbols to help us understand what is shown.

Symbol	Meaning	Symbol	Meaning	Symbol	Meaning
🌲	Coniferous trees	° °	Orchard	W, Spr	Well, Spring
🌳	Non-coniferous trees		Scrub		Water

Map makers also use different colours to make the maps easy to follow.

	Angola		Mozambique		Swaziland
	Botswana		Namibia		Zambia
	Lesotho		South Africa		Zimbabwe
	Malawi				

Map keys

When symbols and colours are used in a map they are usually shown in a key.

The key explains the meaning of the symbols and colours.

The maps in this atlas have their own keys. Read the keys to help you understand the maps.

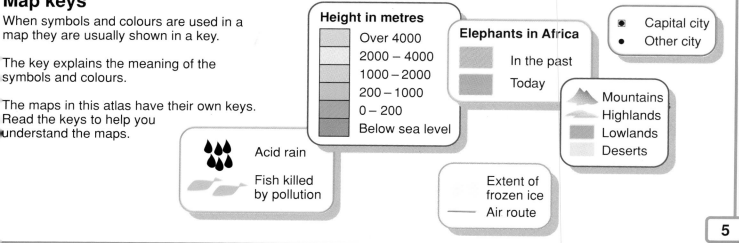

Height in metres
Over 4000
2000 – 4000
1000 – 2000
200 – 1000
0 – 200
Below sea level

Elephants in Africa
In the past
Today

◉ Capital city
● Other city

Mountains
Highlands
Lowlands
Deserts

Acid rain
Fish killed by pollution

Extent of frozen ice
Air route

Using the contents and index

An atlas is a book of maps.

Contents

If you want to find out about a continent or a theme you should first look at the contents page at the front of this atlas.

For example: If you are interested in the mountains and rivers of South America you would look for **South America, Physical** in the contents.

Physical maps tell us about the mountains, rivers and lakes of areas.
Political maps tell us about countries, cities and population.

Cairo Egypt **46 D6**

- name
- page number
- country
- position on page

Index

If you want to find a place such as a river or a city, turn instead to the index at the back of the atlas. Places are listed alphabetically in the index.
For example: If you want to find out about Cairo look under the '**C**' section of the index.

Some places appear on a number of maps in this atlas, eg London. They are listed in the index under the page on which they appear at the largest scale.

Grid references

Most pages have a grid around the edge of the map. The horizontal axis is marked in letters A, B, C, etc. The vertical axis is marked in numbers 1, 2, 3, etc. Using grid references helps us locate places quickly. Cairo can easily be found in grid square **D6**.

Use your skills

Turn to the contents.
On which page will you find:
a) The mountains of Asia?
b) The cities of Africa?
c) The countries of South America?
d) The rivers of Europe?

Turn to the index.
What is the page number and grid reference for:
Dar es Salaam, Berlin, Lima, Washington and Tokyo?
These are the capital cities of which countries?

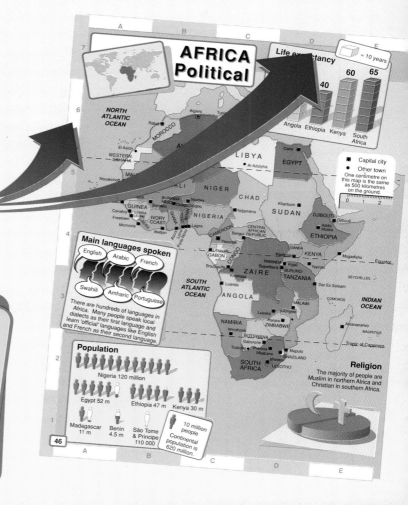

Maps can tell us how far one place is from another. To check distances we must use the map's scale line.

To find the distance from Abergavenny to Monmouth, place your ruler on the map and measure the distance between the two town centres.

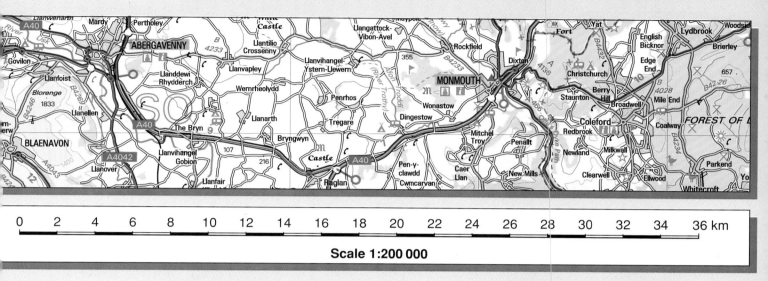

| 0 | 2 | 4 | 6 | 8 | 10 | 12 | 14 | 16 | 18 | 20 | 22 | 24 | 26 | 28 | 30 | 32 | 34 | 36 km |

Scale 1:200 000

measures 10 cm. Check this distance on the scale line. 10 cm is 20 km on the ground. So we know that Abergavenny is 0 km from Monmouth.

eople do not usually travel in straight lines. A better way to measure the distance is to use string. This allows you to follow the oads as they twist and turn. Using string, measure the distance between Abergavenny and Monmouth (a) on the B4233 and) on the A40. Which route is longer and by how much?

ontinental maps are at a much smaller scale. Use your ruler nd scale line to find the distance between Brasilia and La az.

As well as knowing the distance between places we should also know the direction. By using the 8-point compass we can see that La Paz is west of Brasilia.

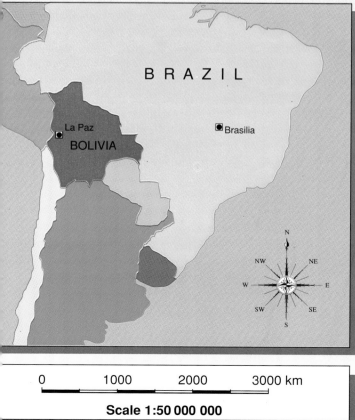

Scale 1:50 000 000

Use your skills
Use the political map of South America on page 50 to find these distances and directions.

Copy and complete the chart. (Distances in km.)

From	To	Distance	Direction
Buenos Aires	Falkland Is		
Montevideo	Buenos Aires		
Santiago	Brasilia		
Montevideo	Lima		
Caracas	Bogota		
La Paz	Caracas		

Latitude and longitude

The world maps in this atlas have a grid reference system which is used all around the world. The earth has had imaginary lines drawn on it to help people locate places.

Latitude

Lines drawn horizontally around the earth are called **lines of latitude**. The first line drawn is where the earth's circumference is greatest. This line is called the **equator**.

Parallel lines are drawn every 15° north and south of the equator (0°). The north pole is at 90° north and the south pole is at 90° south. Lines in between are described as degrees north and south of the equator.

The lines of latitude are then transferred on to a flat map.

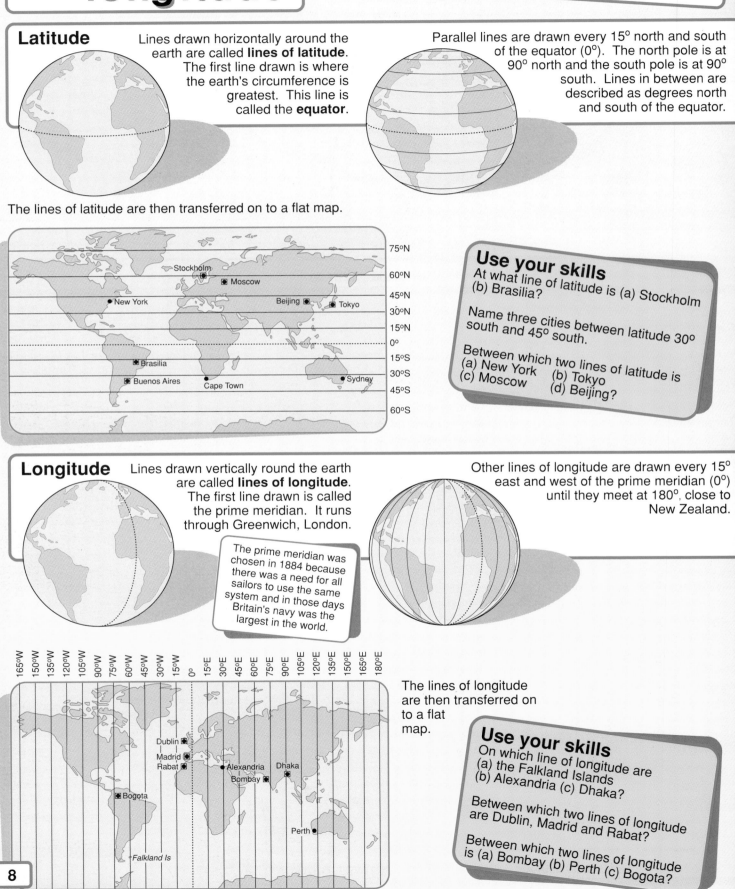

Use your skills

At what line of latitude is (a) Stockholm (b) Brasilia?

Name three cities between latitude 30° south and 45° south.

Between which two lines of latitude is
(a) New York   (b) Tokyo
(c) Moscow   (d) Beijing?

Longitude

Lines drawn vertically round the earth are called **lines of longitude**. The first line drawn is called the prime meridian. It runs through Greenwich, London.

The prime meridian was chosen in 1884 because there was a need for all sailors to use the same system and in those days Britain's navy was the largest in the world.

Other lines of longitude are drawn every 15° east and west of the prime meridian (0°) until they meet at 180°, close to New Zealand.

The lines of longitude are then transferred on to a flat map.

Use your skills

On which line of longitude are
(a) the Falkland Islands
(b) Alexandria (c) Dhaka?

Between which two lines of longitude are Dublin, Madrid and Rabat?

Between which two lines of longitude is (a) Bombay (b) Perth (c) Bogota?

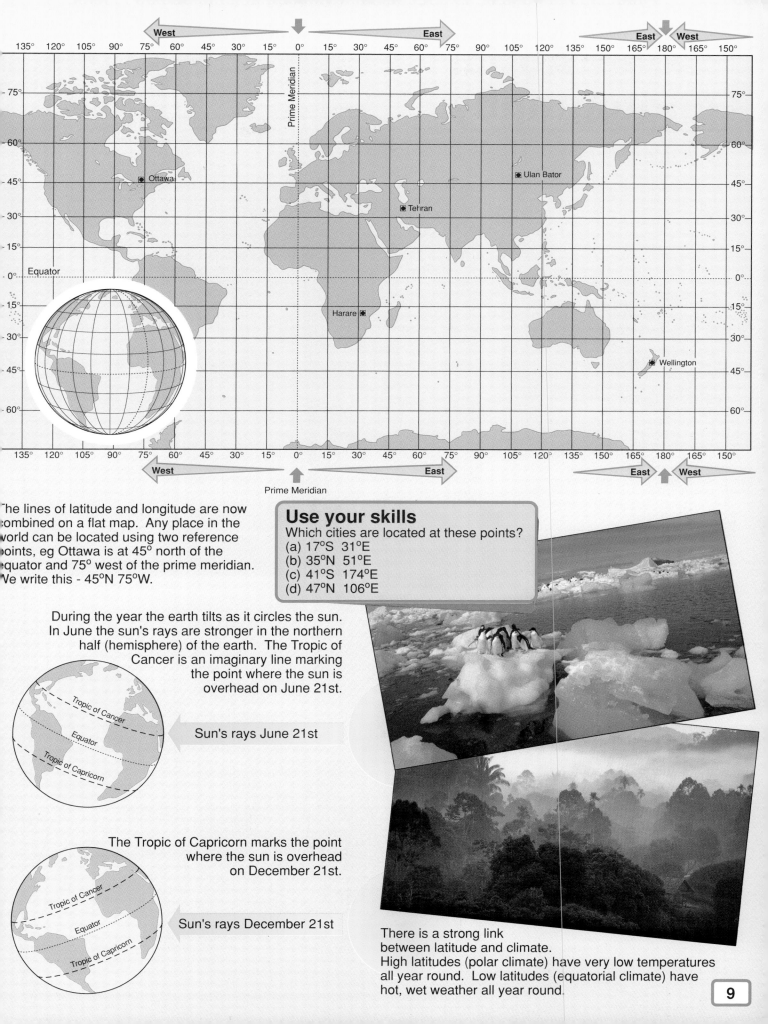

The lines of latitude and longitude are now combined on a flat map. Any place in the world can be located using two reference points, eg Ottawa is at 45° north of the equator and 75° west of the prime meridian. We write this - 45°N 75°W.

Use your skills
Which cities are located at these points?
(a) 17°S 31°E
(b) 35°N 51°E
(c) 41°S 174°E
(d) 47°N 106°E

During the year the earth tilts as it circles the sun. In June the sun's rays are stronger in the northern half (hemisphere) of the earth. The Tropic of Cancer is an imaginary line marking the point where the sun is overhead on June 21st.

Sun's rays June 21st

The Tropic of Capricorn marks the point where the sun is overhead on December 21st.

Sun's rays December 21st

There is a strong link between latitude and climate. High latitudes (polar climate) have very low temperatures all year round. Low latitudes (equatorial climate) have hot, wet weather all year round.

9

Aerial photography

Aerial photographs when used with maps provide us with a great deal of information. Look at the photograph for physical features such as rivers or hills and then find them on the map.

Aerial photographs give us information which is not found on maps.

Use your skills

1. What is the highest building?
2. How is the railway supported?
3. What is the weather like?
4. What season is it?
5. What is growing in the fields?

Aerial photograph

Ordnance Survey map extract

Maps give us information which is not found on aerial photographs.

Use your skills

1. What is this place called?
2. What is the main street called?
3. How many post offices are there?
4. Name the road which passes under the railway bridge.
5. Give the address of a Post Office.

The map has been turned so that it matches the photograph above as closely as possible.

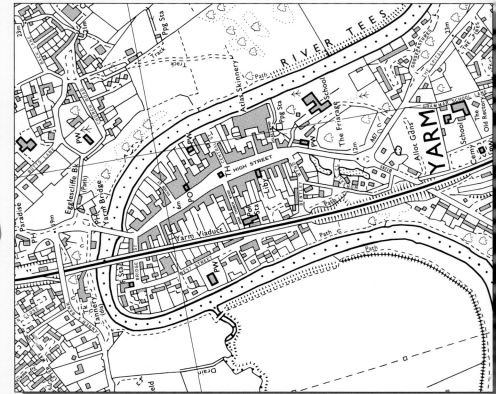

BRITISH ISLES Political

The British Isles - everything named on this map

Great Britain - England, Scotland and Wales

United Kingdom - England, Scotland, Wales and Northern Ireland

Capital city
Other city or town
Country boundary

One centimetre on this map is the same as 50 kilometres on the ground.

0 1 2 3

Shetland Islands

• Lerwick

Orkney Islands

Outer Hebrides

• Stornoway

ATLANTIC OCEAN

• Inverness

SCOTLAND

• Aberdeen

Dundee •
Perth •

Glasgow •

◉ Edinburgh

• Ayr

Derry / Londonderry •

NORTHERN IRELAND

◉ Belfast

• Sligo

Newcastle upon Tyne •
Sunderland •

• Carlisle

Middlesbrough •

North Sea

Isle of Man

◉ Douglas

REPUBLIC OF IRELAND

Galway •

Dublin ◉

Irish Sea

Blackpool •

Bradford • • Leeds

• Kingston upon Hull

Liverpool •

Manchester •
• Sheffield

Holyhead •
Anglesey

• Bangor

Wrexham •

• Nottingham

• Limerick

Norwich •

Wolverhampton • • Birmingham
• Coventry

Peterborough •

Waterford •

Wexford •

Rosslare •

Aberystwyth •

Ipswich •

ENGLAND

Cork •

St George's Channel

WALES

Luton •

Celtic Sea

Swansea •

Newport •

◉ Cardiff

• Bristol

London ◉

Southampton •

Brighton •

• Portsmouth

Exeter •

Plymouth •

Isle of Wight

English Channel

ATLANTIC OCEAN

Isles of Scilly

Channel Islands

11

BRITISH ISLES Physical

N
W E
S

Height in metres

- Over 1000
- 500–1000
- 200–500
- 100–200
- 0–100

Rivers
Lakes
▲ Spot heights

One centimetre on this map is the same as 50 kilometres on the ground.

0 1 2 3

ATLANTIC OCEAN

Northwest Highlands
Moray Firth
Loch Ness
Great Glen
Spey
Dee
Ben Nevis 1344m ▲
Grampian Highlands
Tay
Loch Lomond
Forth
Firth of Forth
Clyde
Firth of Clyde
Nith
Southern Uplands
Tweed
Cheviot Hills
North Sea
Tyne
Wear
Tees
Pennines
North York Moors
Ouse
Humber
The Wash

Donegal Mts
Foyle
Sperrin Mts
Antrim Mts
Belfast Lough
Lough Neagh
Slieve Donard 852m ▲ Mourne Mts
Dundalk Bay
Solway Firth
Cumbrian Mountains
Scafell Pike 977m ▲
Lake Windermere
Morecambe Bay
Mersey

Lough Ree
Boyne
Liffey
Shannon
Lough Derg
Wicklow Mountains
Slaney
Irish Sea
Snowdon 1085m ▲
Caernarfon Bay
Conwy
Llyn Trawsfynydd
Llyn Tegid
Cardigan Bay
Trent
Great Ouse

Carrauntoohil 1041m ▲
Caha Mts
Galty Mts
Blackwater
St George's Channel
Teifi
Cambrian Mountains
Usk
Brecon Beacons
Severn
Avon
Colswold Hills
Chiltern Hills

Celtic Sea
Bristol Channel
Exmoor
Exe
Mendip Hills
Thames
North Downs
South Downs
The Solent

Land's End
Tamar
Dartmoor

English Channel

Ben Nevis
- the highest point in the British Isles at 1 344 m.

The River Shannon is the longest river in the British Isles.

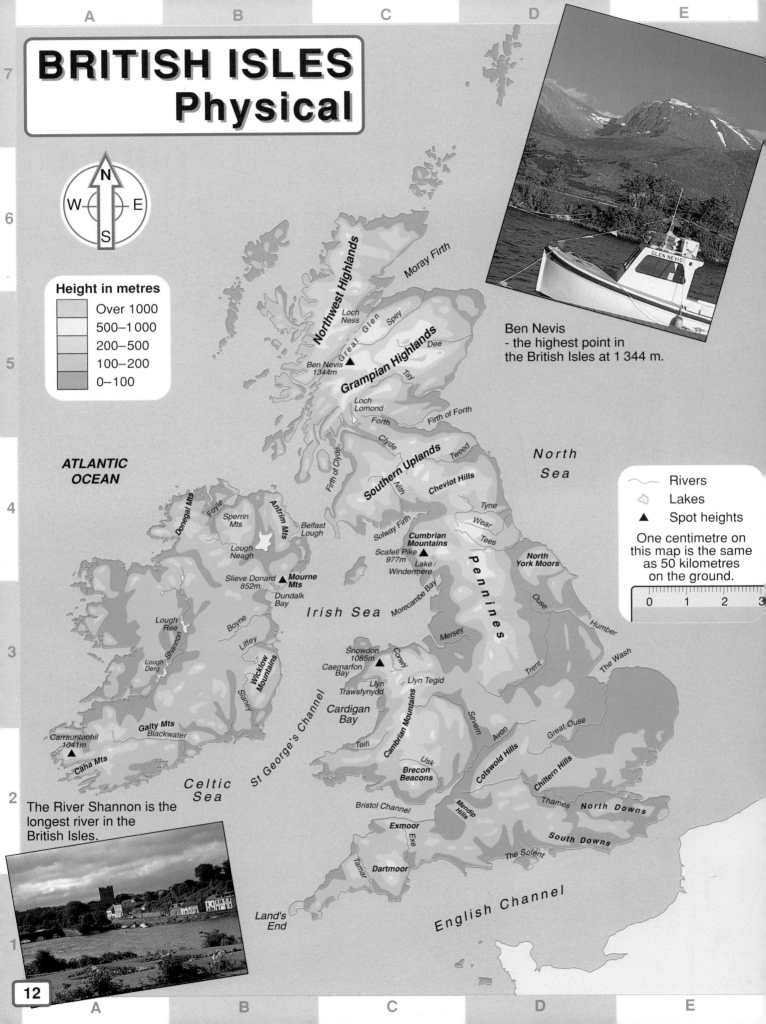

12

The British Isles are in the path of winds which blow across the Atlantic Ocean. These winds are mid-way between warm, moist air from the south and cold dry air from the north. This mixture gives us our very changeable weather.

As the clouds reach the land they start to drop rain. When the clouds rise above high ground they cool and drop even more rain. The west of the British Isles is very wet because the clouds arrive there first. Compare the physical map opposite with the rainfall map. Can you see a connection between high land and heavy rainfall?

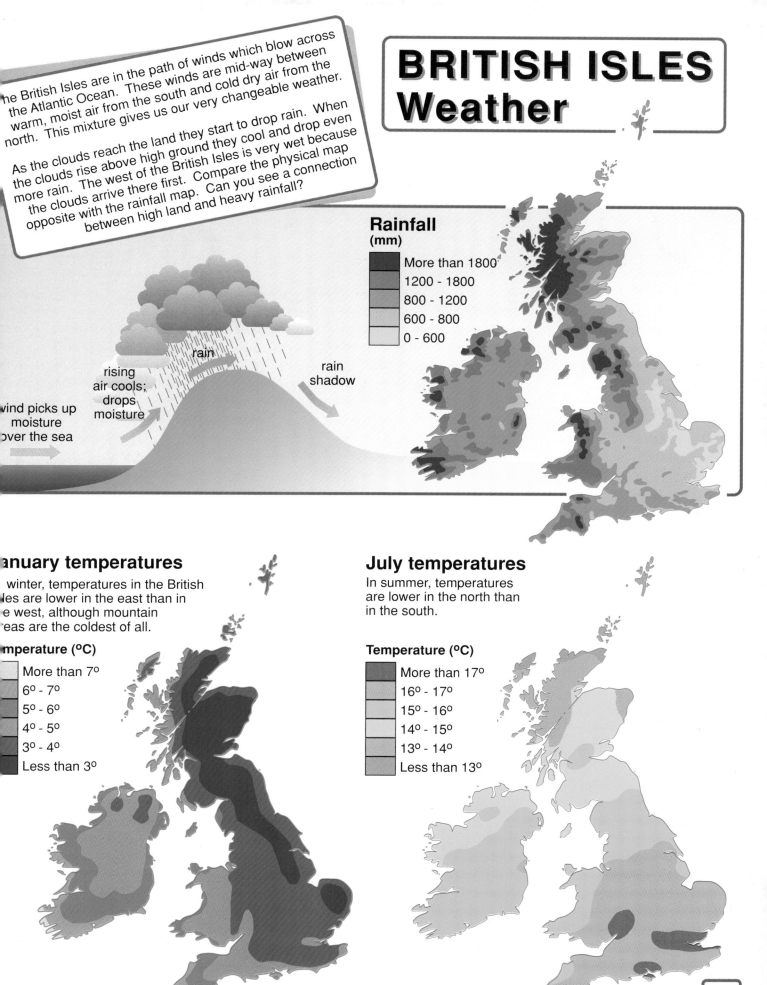

Rainfall
(mm)

More than 1800
1200 - 1800
800 - 1200
600 - 800
0 - 600

rain

rising
air cools;
drops
moisture

rain
shadow

wind picks up
moisture
over the sea

January temperatures

In winter, temperatures in the British Isles are lower in the east than in the west, although mountain areas are the coldest of all.

Temperature (°C)

More than 7°
6° - 7°
5° - 6°
4° - 5°
3° - 4°
Less than 3°

July temperatures

In summer, temperatures are lower in the north than in the south.

Temperature (°C)

More than 17°
16° - 17°
15° - 16°
14° - 15°
13° - 14°
Less than 13°

BRITISH ISLES Communications

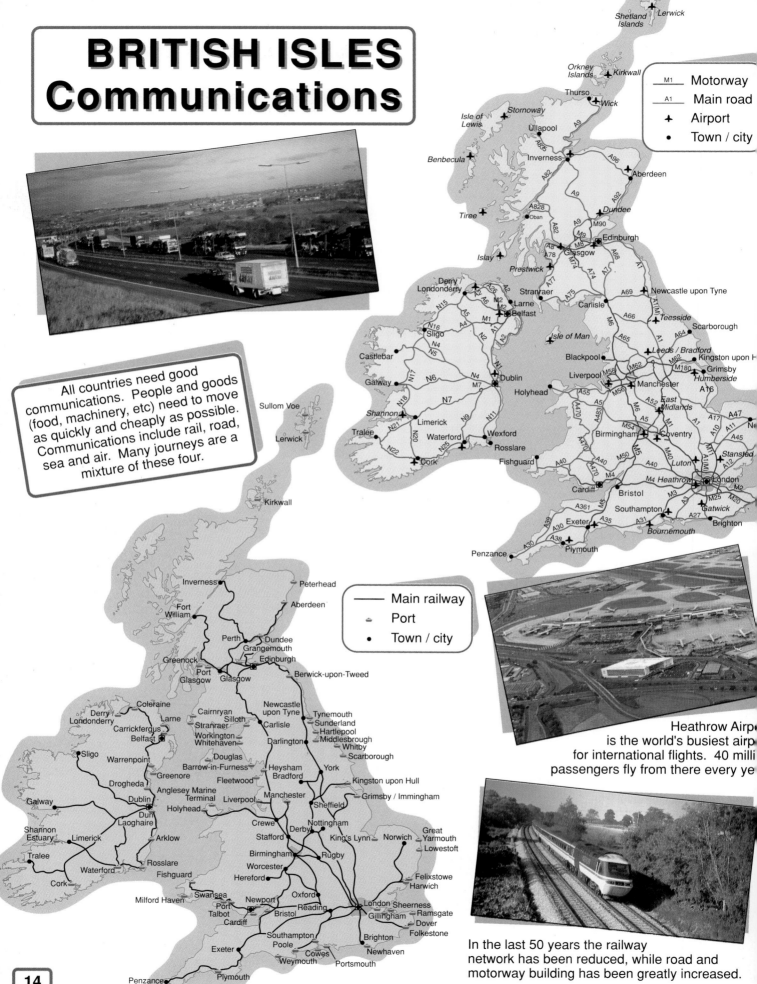

All countries need good communications. People and goods (food, machinery, etc) need to move as quickly and cheaply as possible. Communications include rail, road, sea and air. Many journeys are a mixture of these four.

Legend (roads/air map):
- M1 — Motorway
- A1 — Main road
- ✈ — Airport
- • — Town / city

Legend (railway map):
- — Main railway
- ⌂ — Port
- • — Town / city

Heathrow Airport is the world's busiest airport for international flights. 40 million passengers fly from there every year.

In the last 50 years the railway network has been reduced, while road and motorway building has been greatly increased.

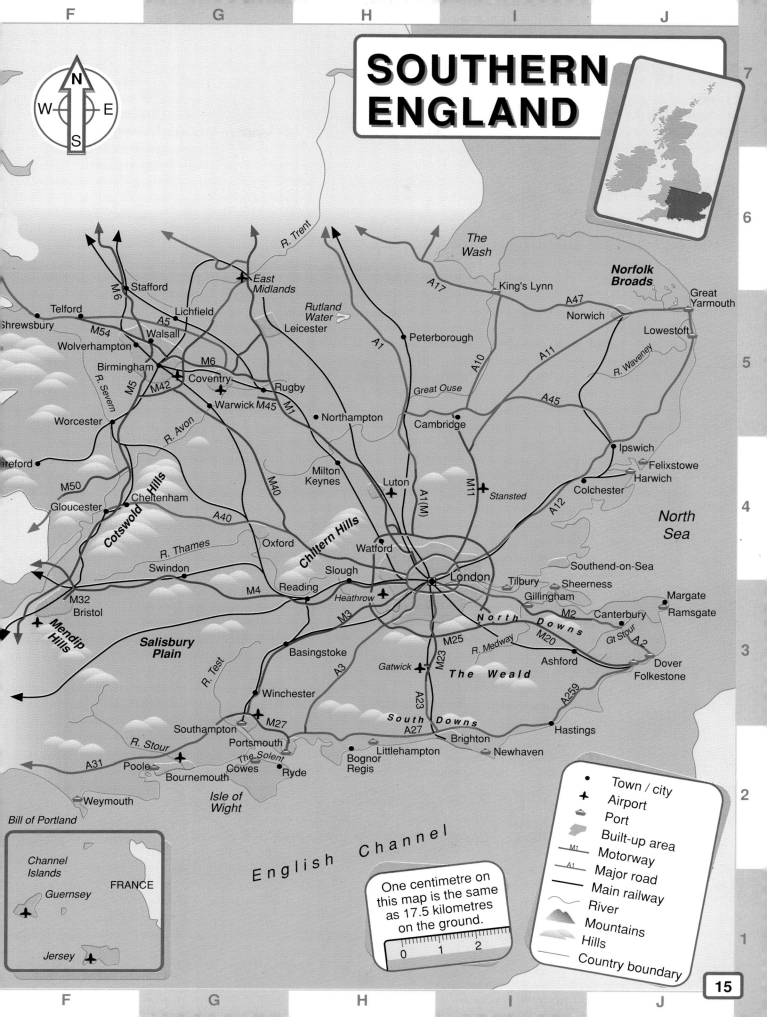

SOUTHERN ENGLAND

N W E S

The Wash

Norfolk Broads

Stafford
Telford
Shrewsbury
M6
M54
Lichfield
A5
East Midlands
Walsall
Wolverhampton
Birmingham
M6
Coventry
Rugby
Warwick M45
M1
M42
M5
R. Severn
R. Avon
Worcester
Hereford
M50
Gloucester
Cheltenham
Cotswold Hills
A40
Oxford
R. Thames
Swindon
M4
Reading
Milton Keynes
Chiltern Hills
Watford
Slough
Heathrow
M40
M32
Bristol
Mendip Hills
Salisbury Plain
R. Test
Winchester
Basingstoke
A3
M3
M27
Southampton
Portsmouth
The Solent
Cowes
Ryde
Isle of Wight
R. Stour
Poole
A31
Bournemouth
Weymouth
Bill of Portland

R. Trent
Rutland Water
Leicester
A1
Peterborough
Northampton
Great Ouse
Cambridge
Luton
A1(M)
M11
Stansted
Ipswich
Felixstowe
Harwich
Colchester
A45
A11
A10
King's Lynn
A17
A47
Norwich
R. Waveney
Lowestoft
Great Yarmouth
A12
North Sea

London
Tilbury
Sheerness
Southend-on-Sea
Gillingham
M2
Canterbury
Margate
Ramsgate
North Downs
Gt Stour
A2
M25
R. Medway
M20
Ashford
Dover
Folkestone
Gatwick
M23
The Weald
A259
A23
South Downs
A27
Brighton
Littlehampton
Newhaven
Hastings
Bognor Regis

English Channel

Channel Islands
FRANCE
Guernsey
Jersey

One centimetre on this map is the same as 17.5 kilometres on the ground.
0 1 2

- Town / city
✈ Airport
⛴ Port
Built-up area
M1 Motorway
A1 Major road
Main railway
River
Mountains
Hills
Country boundary

15

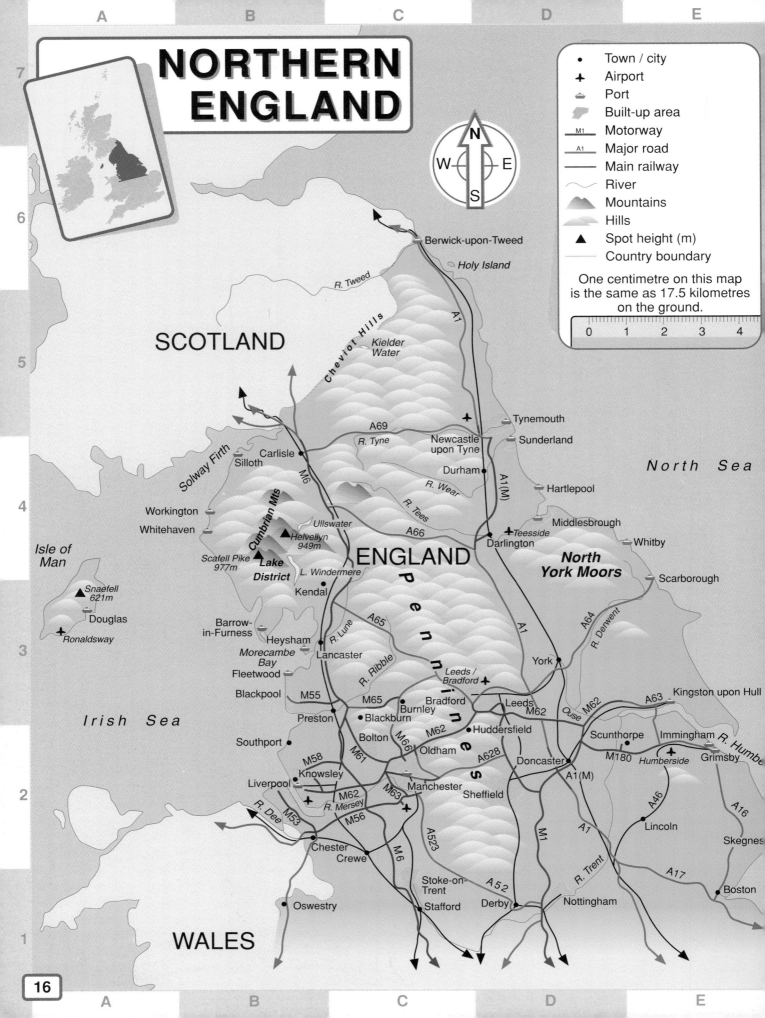

NORTHERN ENGLAND

Legend:
- Town / city
- ✈ Airport
- ⛴ Port
- Built-up area
- M1 Motorway
- A1 Major road
- Main railway
- River
- Mountains
- Hills
- ▲ Spot height (m)
- Country boundary

One centimetre on this map is the same as 17.5 kilometres on the ground.

0 1 2 3 4

N W E S (compass)

SCOTLAND

Berwick-upon-Tweed

Holy Island

R. Tweed

Cheviot Hills

Kielder Water

A1

A69

R. Tyne

Tynemouth

Newcastle upon Tyne

Sunderland

Durham

R. Wear

A1(M)

Hartlepool

North Sea

Carlisle

Silloth

M6

R. Tees

A66

Middlesbrough

Teesside

Darlington

Whitby

Workington

Cumbrian Mts

Ullswater

Helvellyn 949m

ENGLAND

North York Moors

Scarborough

Whitehaven

Scafell Pike 977m

Lake District

L. Windermere

Kendal

Isle of Man

Snaefell 621m

Douglas

Ronaldsway

Barrow-in-Furness

Heysham

Morecambe Bay

Lancaster

R. Lune

A65

R. Ribble

Pennines

A64

R. Derwent

York

Ouse

M62

A63

Kingston upon Hull

Fleetwood

Blackpool

M55

Preston

M65

Burnley

Blackburn

Bradford

Leeds / Bradford

Leeds

M62

Huddersfield

R. Humber

Immingham

Scunthorpe

M180

Humberside

Grimsby

Irish Sea

Southport

M58

Knowsley

M61

Bolton

M62

Oldham

A628

Doncaster

A1(M)

Liverpool

M62

R. Mersey

M63

Manchester

Sheffield

A46

Lincoln

Skegnes

A16

M53

R. Dee

M56

Chester

Crewe

M6

A523

Stoke-on-Trent

Stafford

A52

Derby

Nottingham

R. Trent

A1

M1

A17

Boston

Oswestry

WALES

16

Traffic congestion in and around large towns has increased year by year. Different solutions are being tried around the country. Bus lanes allow buses to travel faster than cars. This should attract more passengers on to the buses.
In Manchester a new tram-way has been laid. Large numbers of people can be taken quickly and cleanly through the city centre. Trams do not give off exhaust fumes, they run on electricity.
Attempts to attract more people to use the train depend on clean, comfortable, fast and reliable services.

arge thermal power stations have been built in the coal mining eas of Yorkshire and the east Midlands. Many jobs depend them. The pollution that they cause means that their future under threat.

Fact file
England

Population	47 873 300
Highest mountain	Scafell Pike 977 m (3162 ft)
Longest river	Severn 354 km (220 miles)
Largest lake	Windermere 15 sq km (5.5 sq miles)

Interesting facts:
The River Severn has its source in Wales.

The Norfolk Broads is a habitat for many rare birds and insects. Some, like the Swallowtail Butterfly, live only in the Norfolk Broads. This habitat is in danger. Chemical pollution from farms and an increasing number of tourists threaten this environment.

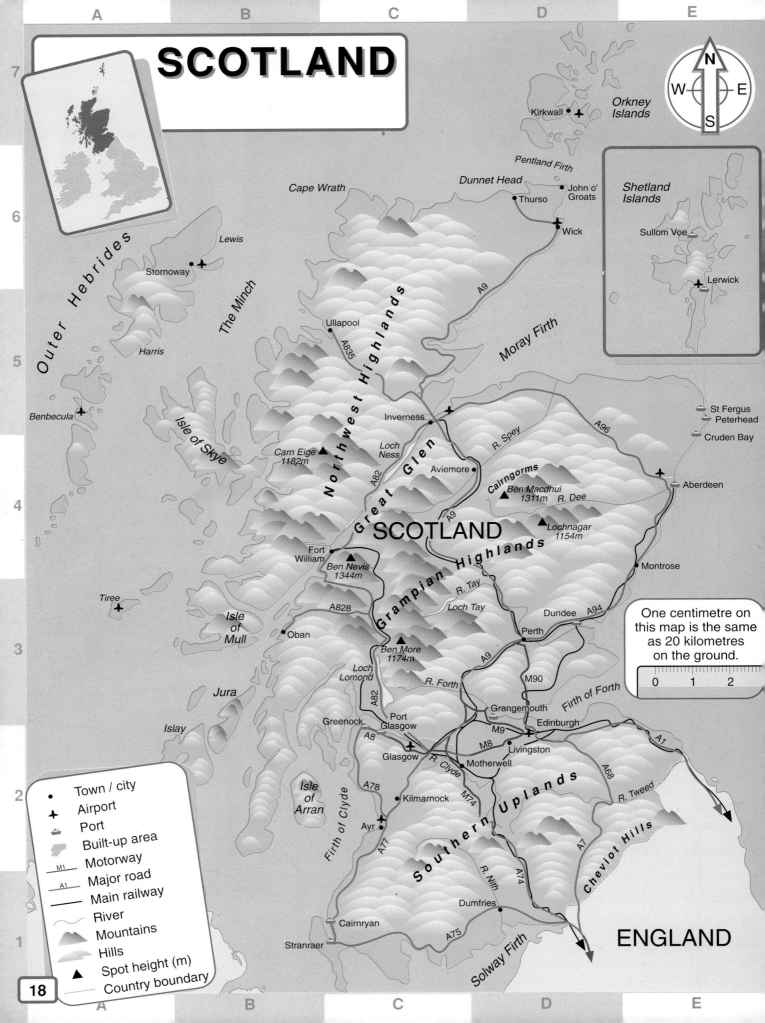

SCOTLAND

N
W · E
S

Orkney Islands

Kirkwall ✈
Pentland Firth
Dunnet Head
Thurso • John o' Groats
Wick ⚓
A9
Moray Firth

Shetland Islands
Sullom Voe
Lerwick ✈ ⚓

Cape Wrath

Lewis
Stornoway • ✈
Outer Hebrides
Harris
The Minch

Ullapool
A835
Northwest Highlands

Inverness ✈
Loch Ness
Great Glen
A82
R. Spey
Aviemore
Cairngorms
Ben Macdhui 1311m ▲
R. Dee
A96
St Fergus
Peterhead
Cruden Bay

Benbecula ✈
Isle of Skye
Carn Eige 1182m ▲

SCOTLAND
A9
Lochnagar 1154m ▲
Aberdeen ✈

Fort William
Ben Nevis 1344m ▲
Grampian Highlands
R. Tay
Montrose

Tiree ✈
A828
Loch Tay
Dundee A94

Isle of Mull
Oban •
Ben More 1174m ▲
Perth •
A9
M90
Firth of Forth

Jura
Loch Lomond
R. Forth
Grangemouth
Edinburgh ✈
A1

Islay
A82
Port Glasgow
Greenock •
M9
M8 Livingston
A68
R. Tweed

Glasgow •
A8
R. Clyde
Motherwell
Cheviot Hills

Isle of Arran
A78
Kilmarnock •
M74
Southern Uplands
A7

Firth of Clyde
Ayr • ✈
A77
R. Nith
A74

Cairnryan ⚓
Dumfries •
A75
ENGLAND

Stranraer •
Solway Firth

One centimetre on this map is the same as 20 kilometres on the ground.

0 1 2

Legend
- • Town / city
- ✈ Airport
- ⚓ Port
- Built-up area
- M1 Motorway
- A1 Major road
- Main railway
- River
- ▲ Mountains
- Hills
- ▲ Spot height (m)
- Country boundary

life on the cool, wet, western islands has always been hard. Today many islands have been deserted. People have moved to the mainland to find jobs and a more comfortable life. A way of life that has existed for generations is coming to an end.

Oil and gas were discovered beneath the North Sea in the 1970s. Today much of the oil is piped to Sullom Voe in the Shetlands and to Cruden Bay near Aberdeen. The main gas lines run to St Fergus north of Aberdeen. Many jobs have been created in the oil and gas industries.

Many people in Scotland are unhappy at being governed from London and want more control over what happens to their country. That could include deciding how oil and gas earnings should be spent.

Fact file
Scotland

Population	5 102 400
Highest mountain	Ben Nevis 1 344 m (4 406 ft)
Longest river	Tay 188 km (117 miles)
Largest lake	Loch Lomond 70 sq km (27.5 sq miles)

Interesting facts:

The oldest rocks in the British Isles are in the West Highlands and Western Isles. They are almost 3 000 million years old.

Tourism is an important industry employing many thousands of people throughout Scotland. Glasgow, Scotland's largest city, is now a major tourist attraction. This has helped provide work for people who lost their jobs when older industries were run down.

Tourism needs to be managed. If too many tourists visit the wilder parts of Scotland, they could pose a threat to the wildlife which lives there. Golden eagles and wildcats were once common throughout Britain. It is vitally important that they continue to survive in the Scottish Highlands and that the tourist industry operates in harmony with the natural environment.

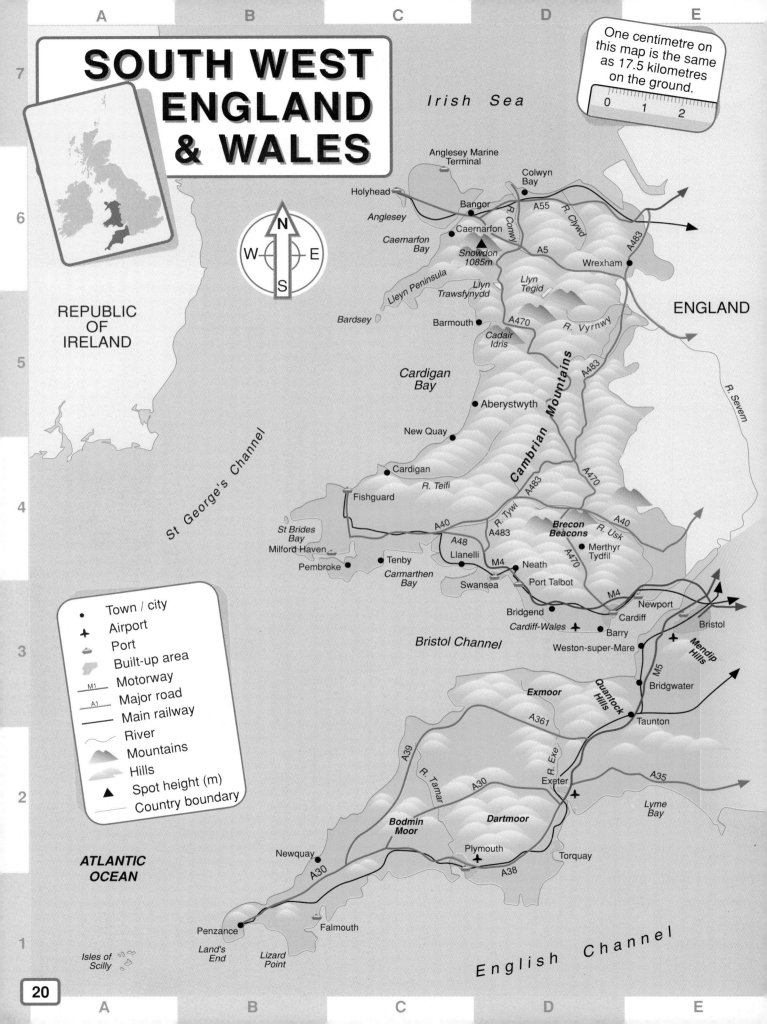

SOUTH WEST ENGLAND & WALES

One centimetre on this map is the same as 17.5 kilometres on the ground.

0   1   2

Irish Sea

REPUBLIC OF IRELAND

ENGLAND

N
W   E
S

Anglesey Marine Terminal

Colwyn Bay

Holyhead

Bangor

A55   R. Clywd

Anglesey

Caernarfon

A5

Caernarfon Bay

A483

Snowdon 1085m

Wrexham

Lleyn Peninsula

Llyn Trawsfynydd

Llyn Tegid

Bardsey

Barmouth

R. Vyrnwy

Cadair Idris

A470

Cardigan Bay

Cambrian Mountains

A483

R. Severn

Aberystwyth

New Quay

A470

Cardigan

R. Teifi

A483

St George's Channel

Fishguard

A40

R. Tywi

Brecon Beacons

A40

St Brides Bay

A48

A483

R. Usk

Milford Haven

Llanelli

Merthyr Tydfil

Pembroke

Tenby

M4

Neath

A470

Carmarthen Bay

Swansea

Port Talbot

M4

Newport

Bridgend

Cardiff

Bristol

Cardiff-Wales

Barry

Bristol Channel

Weston-super-Mare

Mendip Hills

M5

Exmoor

Quantock Hills

Bridgwater

Legend

● Town / city
✈ Airport
⚓ Port
▨ Built-up area
━M1━ Motorway
─A1─ Major road
━━ Main railway
〜 River
⛰ Mountains
◠ Hills
▲ Spot height (m)
⋯ Country boundary

A361

Taunton

R. Exe

A35

A39

R. Tamar

A30

Exeter

Lyme Bay

ATLANTIC OCEAN

Bodmin Moor

Dartmoor

Newquay

A30

Plymouth

Torquay

A38

Penzance

Isles of Scilly

Land's End

Falmouth

Lizard Point

English Channel

There are no jobs here, so we are moving to London.

WALES | ENGLAND

We can afford a second home; we've decided to buy one in Wales.

For many years Welsh language and culture were in decline. Now attempts are being made to change this. Welsh-speaking schools are increasing and TV programmes in Welsh are more common. Welsh is once again a valued language. However young Welsh speaking people continue to leave Wales in order to find jobs. At the same time, English speakers buy homes in Wales for holidays or retirement. This demand for second homes drives up the prices of houses, making it even harder for young Welsh people to buy a home in the area where they were born.

Wales was once a major slate- and coal-producing country. Slate quarrying declined earlier this century, as more homes were built using tiles instead of slate. In the 1980s and 1990s many coal pits were closed. Thousands were thrown out of work. Efforts have been made to attract new industries to Wales.

Fact file
Wales

Population   2 881 400

Highest mountain   Snowdon 1085 m (3561 ft)

Longest river   Usk 105 km (65 miles)

Largest lake   Llyn Tegid 4.5 sq km (1.5 sq miles)

Interesting facts:

Llyn Tegid is the largest *natural* lake. Larger lakes have been formed by dams.

Tourists from all over the world are attracted to Snowdonia. The castles along the coast are among the finest in Europe. The scenery of the mountains is breathtaking. Wild goats and rare plants can be seen on the higher, wilder slopes. Tourists are encouraged to respect this natural environment so that future generations will also enjoy it.

IRELAND

One centimetre on this map is the same as 20 kilometres on the ground.

0   1   2

N
W — E
S

ATLANTIC OCEAN

Giant's Causeway

Coleraine

R. Foyle

Derry / Londonderry

Strabane
R. Mourne

Donegal Mts

N15

Donegal

Sperrin Mts

Antrim Mts

A2

R. Bann

Ballymena

A6

M2

Larne

Carrickfergus

Belfast Lough

Donegal Bay

Omagh

Lower L. Erne

NORTHERN IRELAND

Lough Neagh

M2

Belfast

Bangor

Lisburn

R. Lagan

Strangford Lough

M1

A1

A2

Sligo

N16

A4

Upper L. Erne

Armagh

N2

R. Bann

Mourne Mts

▲ *Slieve Donard* 852m

Ballina

Lough Conn

Lough Key

Lough Gara

Lough Allen

Lough Oughter

Crossmaglen

Warrenpoint

Dundalk

Greenore

Dundalk Bay

Castlebar

Westport

N17

Lough Carra

N5

N4

R. Erne

Lough Gowna

R. Boyne

N1

Drogheda

Irish Sea

Lough Mask

Lough Corrib

Lough Ree

Athlone

N6

N4

Dublin

Dublin Bay

Galway

N6

R. Shannon

REPUBLIC OF IRELAND

N7

Portlaoise

R. Liffey

M7

Dun Laoghaire

Galway Bay

Lough Derg

Wicklow Mountains

Wicklow

N18

Shannon

Shannon Estuary

Limerick

Thurles

N9

R. Slaney

N11

Arklow

N21

N20

Galty Mts

R. Blackwater

New Ross

Waterford

Wexford

Rosslare

Rosslare Harbour

Tralee

▲ *Carrauntoohil* 1041m

N22

Cork

R. Lee

N25

St George's Channel

Caha Mts

Mizen Head

Celtic Sea

Legend

• Town / city		▬ Main railway	
✈ Airport		∿ River	
⛴ Port		⛰ Mountains	
Built-up area		Hills	
M1 Motorway		▲ Spot height (m)	
A1/N1 Major road		Country boundary	

22

Emigration from Ireland

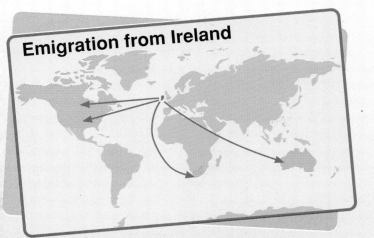

Irish communities are found throughout the English speaking world. In the USA, for example, they are proud to be known as 'Irish Americans'. Over the past 200 years Ireland has seen its people leave to start new lives in other places. This is still a serious issue in Ireland today. If young people leave they take skills, ambition and energy with them. Ways must be found to provide interesting, well paid jobs which will reduce emigration.

Population of Ireland in the 19th century

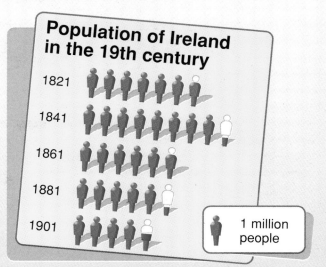

1821	
1841	
1861	
1881	
1901	

1 million people

The potato blight of 1846 led to 1 million people dying and 1 million emigrating. By 1870 nearly 2 million Irish born people lived in the USA and threequarters of a million lived in Scotland, England and Wales.

Farming is a major industry in Ireland. The mild climate with its regular rainfall is ideal for the grass crops on which sheep and cattle feed.

The rivers and loughs of Ireland are famous. Anglers from all around the world are among the many tourists who visit Ireland every year.

For many years the people of Belfast have lived with sectarian violence between extremist 'Loyalists' who want Ulster to remain part of the United Kingdom and extremist 'Republicans' who want British rule to end.

Fact file
Ireland

Population	5 089 400
Highest mountain	Carrauntoohil 1 041 m (3 414 ft)
Longest river	Shannon 386 km (240 miles)
Largest lake	Lough Neagh 382 sq km (147 sq miles)

Interesting facts:
About 3.5 million people live in the Republic and 1.5 million live in Northern Ireland (Ulster).

British Isles index

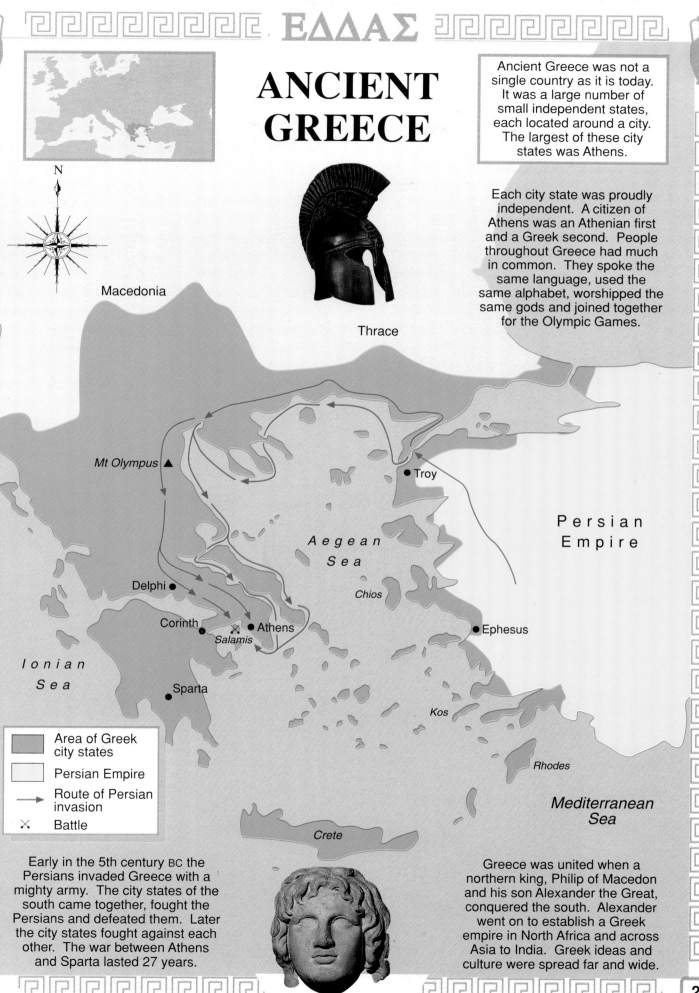

ANCIENT GREECE

ΕΛΛΑΣ

Ancient Greece was not a single country as it is today. It was a large number of small independent states, each located around a city. The largest of these city states was Athens.

Each city state was proudly independent. A citizen of Athens was an Athenian first and a Greek second. People throughout Greece had much in common. They spoke the same language, used the same alphabet, worshipped the same gods and joined together for the Olympic Games.

Macedonia

Thrace

N

Mt Olympus ▲

● Troy

Persian Empire

Aegean Sea

Chios

Delphi ●

Corinth ● ✕ ● Athens
Salamis

● Ephesus

Ionian Sea

Sparta ●

Kos

Rhodes

Mediterranean Sea

	Area of Greek city states
	Persian Empire
→	Route of Persian invasion
✕	Battle

Crete

Early in the 5th century BC the Persians invaded Greece with a mighty army. The city states of the south came together, fought the Persians and defeated them. Later the city states fought against each other. The war between Athens and Sparta lasted 27 years.

Greece was united when a northern king, Philip of Macedon and his son Alexander the Great, conquered the south. Alexander went on to establish a Greek empire in North Africa and across Asia to India. Greek ideas and culture were spread far and wide.

INVADERS · AND · SETTLERS

The map shows the routes taken by invaders and settlers from their homelands to Britain. It covers the period from 55 BC when Julius Caesar landed in Britain, to the year AD 900 when the Viking invasions were almost at an end.

Invasions
→ Roman
→ Anglo-Saxon (5th-7th centuries A...)
→ Viking (AD 793-90...)

Shetland Is
800   700
Orkney Is
NORWAY
SCOTLAND
North Sea
800-840
793
JUTES
DENMARK
ANGLES
IRELAND
Isle of Man
794
867
841
WALES   ENGLAND
834
SAXONS
FRISIANS
800
855
840
Caesar (55 BC)
Claudius (AD 43)

ATLANTIC OCEAN

Roman Britain

Although Julius Caesar visited Britain in 55 BC , the Romans did not stay. A full Roman invasion under Emperor Claudius took place in AD 43.

The Roman Empire
Rome
Roman Empire

Scotland was always a problem for the Romans. They built Hadrian's Wall to keep the northern tribes out of their newly conquered land. Later they built a second wall, the Antonine Wall, but they never had complete control over Scotland.

Inchtuthil
Inveresk
ANTONINE WALL
HADRIAN'S WALL
South Shields

Hadrian's Wall was 117 km long and 6.5 m high. It had a large fort every 8 km and a smaller one every 1.5 km.

Carlisle

— Roman road
- - Roman wall
● Roman town

York   Brough
Chester   Lincoln
FOSSE WAY
Leicester
Wroxeter
WATLING STREET
ERMINE STREET
Caistor

Some Britons welcomed Roman rule. Others did not. The most important rebellion took place in AD 61 when the Iceni tribe, led by Boudicca, fought and almost defeated the Roman army.

Gloucester
Caerleon   Cirencester   St Albans   London   Colchester
Bath   Silchester   Richborough
Chichester   Dover
Exeter   Dorchester

Tribes of Ancient Britain

VACOMAGI
CALEDONII   TAEXALI
VENICONES
DUMNONII   VOTADINI
SELGOVAE
NOVANTAE
BRIGANTES
PARISI
ORDOVICES   CORITANI
CORNOVII
ICENI
SILURES   CATUVELLAUNI   TRINOVANTES
DOBUNII
DUMNONII   ATREBATES   CANTIUM

Roman soldiers from Britain went to fight in continental Europe i... AD 407. Those left behind could not defend Britain from the new invaders. The Roman Emperor told the British that he could no longer protect them. From AD 409 the British were on their own.

The Anglo-Saxons

Anglo-Saxon kingdoms

The name 'Anglo-Saxon' is used to describe the peoples who came from the coastal parts of what we now call the Netherlands, North Germany and Denmark.

England was not a single country, it was divided into several kingdoms each ruled over by different Anglo-Saxon kings and queens.

The word England comes from Angle Land – but the invaders were not only Angles. There were also Saxons, Jutes and Frisians.

In some areas the invaders replaced or married the native Britons. In other areas a small number of Anglo-Saxons ruled over the local British.

PICTS

Northumbria

BRITONS

Offa's Dyke

Mercia

East Anglia

Essex

Kent

Wessex

Sussex

The native British were pushed to the west of Britain. Only Wales remained unconquered. From AD 784 to AD 796 a great ditch was dug on the orders of King Offa of Mercia. It marked the border between Wales and Mercia. You can still visit parts of Offa's Dyke today.

The Vikings

Viking invaders came to the British Isles from Denmark and Norway. Danish Vikings attacked and settled in eastern and southern England. Norwegians settled in the Scottish islands, the Isle of Man, parts of western Scotland, England and Wales and coastal areas of Ireland.

Shetland Is

Orkney Is

Vikings ruled over most of northern and eastern England. Their own customs and laws were followed there, so the area was known as the Danelaw.

Main areas of Viking settlement

Isle of Man

IRELAND

Danelaw

WALES

Anglo-Saxons

Wessex

In Ireland, King Brian Boru of Munster led the Irish fightback against the Vikings. In England King Alfred the Great of Wessex stopped their advance.

27

TUDOR AND STUART TIMES
The Armada

In 16th century Europe, there were many conflicts between Catholics and Protestants. Elizabeth I of England was a Protestant. She became Queen on the death of her half sister Queen Mary. Mary was a Catholic and married to King Philip II of Spain. Philip was angry with Elizabeth. He believed she was treating Catholics badly in England and that she was helping Protestants in the Netherlands which was a part of his Empire.

(4) Storms drove many Spanish ships on to the shores of Ireland. Survivors were killed as they came ashore because the English feared the Spanish Catholic sailors might join the Irish Catholic people and fight against the English.
When the remaining Spanish ships reached home, so many men had died and the fleet was so badly damaged that the invasion of England was no longer possible.

15 Aug 1588

(3) The Spanish decided not to risk another battle in the Channel but to try to reach home by sailing around Scotland and Ireland.

North Sea

SCOTLAND

IRELAND

WALES

ENGLAND

London ◉

8 Aug 1588
Gravelines
Calais

SPANISH NETHERLANDS

Spanish Army

(2) As the Spanish sailed through the Channel they fought the English navy. The Armada had to wait at Calais because the Spanish army was not ready. The English fleet attacked. The next day a great battle took place at Gravelines. Many Spanish ships were damaged.

19 July 1588

English *Channel*

ATLANTIC OCEAN

Legend
	Area under English control
	Area under Spanish control
	Route of Spanish Armada
	Spanish ships
	English ships
	Area of fighting
★	Battle
	Storm

La Coruña

Santander
Sept - Oct 1588
70 ships

◉ Madrid

SPAIN

PORTUGAL

Lisbon
May 1588
150 ships

Cadiz ●

(1) Philip had a large army in the Netherlands. He sent a great fleet of ships (Armada) from Spain. The plan was to meet the army and carry it across the English Channel, ready for an attack on London.

EXPLORATION AND ENCOUNTERS
1450 to 1550

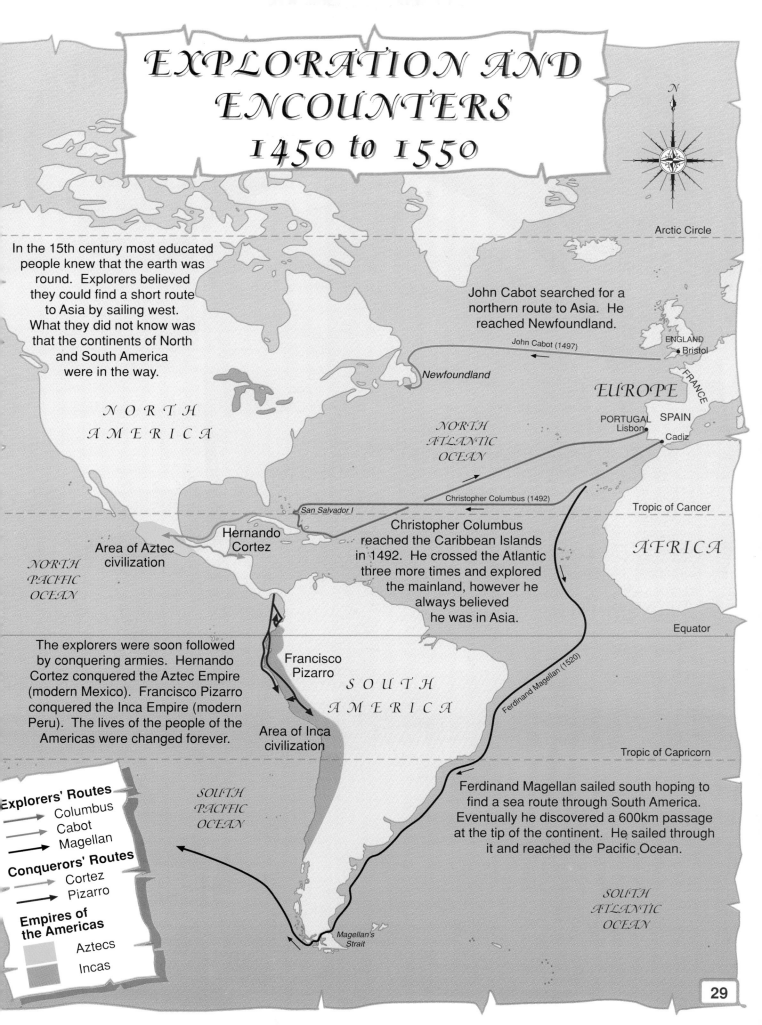

In the 15th century most educated people knew that the earth was round. Explorers believed they could find a short route to Asia by sailing west. What they did not know was that the continents of North and South America were in the way.

John Cabot searched for a northern route to Asia. He reached Newfoundland.

John Cabot (1497)

Newfoundland

NORTH AMERICA

NORTH ATLANTIC OCEAN

EUROPE

ENGLAND
• Bristol

FRANCE

PORTUGAL   SPAIN
Lisbon•   • Cadiz

Christopher Columbus (1492)

San Salvador I

Christopher Columbus reached the Caribbean Islands in 1492. He crossed the Atlantic three more times and explored the mainland, however he always believed he was in Asia.

Tropic of Cancer

AFRICA

Area of Aztec civilization

Hernando Cortez

NORTH PACIFIC OCEAN

Equator

The explorers were soon followed by conquering armies. Hernando Cortez conquered the Aztec Empire (modern Mexico). Francisco Pizarro conquered the Inca Empire (modern Peru). The lives of the people of the Americas were changed forever.

Francisco Pizarro

SOUTH AMERICA

Ferdinand Magellan (1520)

Area of Inca civilization

Tropic of Capricorn

SOUTH PACIFIC OCEAN

Ferdinand Magellan sailed south hoping to find a sea route through South America. Eventually he discovered a 600km passage at the tip of the continent. He sailed through it and reached the Pacific Ocean.

SOUTH ATLANTIC OCEAN

Explorers' Routes
Columbus
Cabot
Magellan

Conquerors' Routes
Cortez
Pizarro

Empires of the Americas
Aztecs
Incas

Magellan's Strait

Arctic Circle

N

29

VICTORIAN BRITAIN

Victoria became Queen in 1837. She died in 1901. Great changes took place in Britain during her reign.

Railways
— Built before 1841
— Built by 1850

In the early part of the 19th century most goods travelled by canal. This was slow and affected by ice in winter and water short in summer. The railways changed all The world's first public steam railway between Stockton and Darlington in 18

The first inter-city railway ran between Liverpool and Manchester in 1830 The map shows the great increase in railways up to 1850.

The population of London rose from 2 685 000 in 1851 to 6 586 000 in 1901. It was the largest city in the world.

City population

1851 | 1901

The railways and factories needed coal for fuel. Coal production in Victorian Britain increased enormously

Growth of other British cities

Thousands of people

800
700
600
500
400
300
200
100
0

Belfast, Birmingham, Bristol, Dublin, Edinburgh, Glasgow, Liverpool, Manchester, Sheffield

Railways made trade quicker and cheaper. British cities grew rapidly as people moved there to work in factories and mills. The chart shows the population of Britain's main cities in 1851 and 1901.

Coal production

1840
34 200 tons

1901
222 562 tons

Map labels: Aberdeen, Montrose, Arbroath, Perth, Dundee, Glasgow, Edinburgh, Berwick, Ayr, Hawick, Newcastle, Carlisle, Durham, Stockton, Middlesbrough, Darlington, Scarborough, Lancaster, Leeds, York, Hull, Preston, Manchester, Liverpool, Grimsby, Birkenhead, Sheffield, Holyhead, Lincoln, Chester, Crewe, Nottingham, Derby, Stafford, Leicester, Shrewsbury, Peterborough, Yarmouth, Birmingham, Rugby, Norwich, Ely, Cambridge, Gloucester, Oxford, Colchester, Swansea, Whitstable, London, Cardiff, Canterbury, Bristol, Guildford, Gosport, Lewes, Dover, Salisbury, St Leonards, Southampton, Dorchester, Portsmouth, Brighton, Newhaven, Exeter, Plymouth

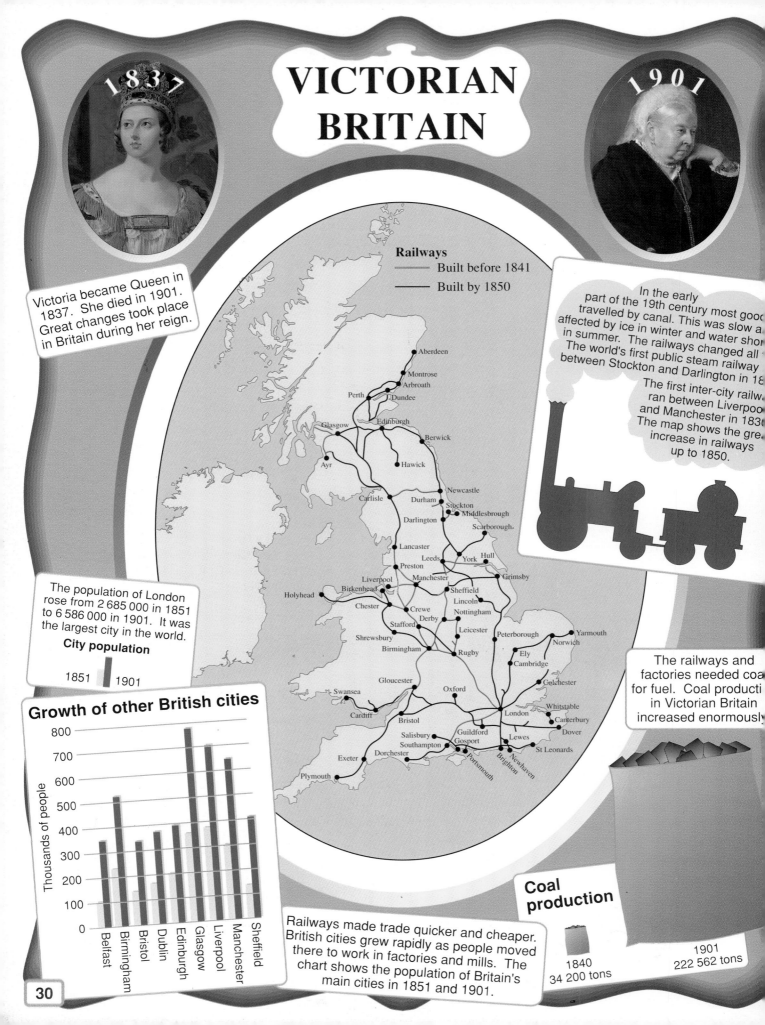

THE BRITISH EMPIRE

Britain, like other European countries, began to establish an empire in the 16th and 17th centuries. Some parts of the Empire rebelled against rule from London. The USA fought and declared its independence in 1776.

The growth of empire continued into the 19th century. In 1901 the British Empire covered one quarter of the world's surface. One in four of the world's population was ruled over by Queen Victoria.

CANADA

UNITED KINGDOM

GIBRALTAR

CYPRUS

MALTA

BALUCHISTAN

UPPER BURMA

BERMUDA

BAHAMAS

EGYPT

INDIA

BURMA

BRITISH HONDURAS

JAMAICA

Leeward Is
BARBADOS
TRINIDAD

NIGERIA

ANGLO EGYPTIAN SUDAN

BRITISH SOMALILAND

MALAYA

BORNEO

BRITISH GUIANA

GAMBIA
SIERRA LEONE

GOLD COAST

BUGANDA

BRITISH EAST AFRICA

Ascension

NORTH RHODESIA

NYASALAND

PAPUA NEW GUINEA

FIJI

St Helena

SOUTH RHODESIA

AUSTRALIA

BECHUANALAND

NATAL
TRANSVAAL
ORANGE FREE STATE

CAPE PROVINCE

The British Empire at the end of Queen Victoria's reign

Falkland Is

NEW ZEALAND

Georgia

Most of the population of countries like Canada, Australia and New Zealand were descended from British settlers. These countries made many of their own decisions.

Some countries, like India, had been part of the Empire for a long time. Most of the soldiers and officials in British India were Indians.

In Africa much of the Empire was 'new', brought under British control in the second half of Queen Victoria's reign.

ANCIENT EGYPT

Mediterranean Sea

Nile Delta

Alexandria

LOWER EGYPT

Giza

Memphis

El-Faiyûm

Bhar Yusaf

Nile

Pyramid and sphinx at Giza

Temple of Amun at Karnak

Eastern Desert

Red Sea

UPPER

Karnak
Thebes

EGYPT

N

Aswan

The Inundation

August and September (flooding)

January to April (harvesting)

The Nile was at its lowest level in June. It rose in July and flooded in August and September. In October and November, as the water level fell, the crops were sown. The main crops were cereals for bread, barley for beer, vegetables, fruit especially dates and sesame for oil. These were harvested from January to April before the next flood.

Abu Simbel

Abu Simbel, Temple of Rameses II

River

Fertile strip

Land below sea level

WHOSE OCEAN?

The sea covers more than 70% of the Earth. The largest ocean is the Pacific which is four times bigger than Asia. The seas are rich in life but today that life is under threat.

The Mediterranean Sea is badly polluted. Most of the pollution comes from the land. Chemicals used in farming, industrial waste and sewage all pour into the sea.

Species at risk

Whale numbers have been greatly reduced by hunting. Campaigns from conservationists have reduced, but not stopped, whaling. Other species such as haddock, herring and mackerel have also been overfished.

Six million tonnes of oil enter the Earth's oceans every year. Some of this is accidental but much is caused by oil tankers 'washing-out' their tanks.

Large factory ships from Japan and Europe travel great distances to fish in the seas off West Africa. These ships can handle up to 1 000 tonnes of fish a day. Most of this fish will be used as fertiliser on farms.

Local fishing people can only watch as their traditional catch is taken far away.

Fishing with narrow-mesh nets in the Indian and Pacific Oceans has killed many dolphins and porpoises. Today these nets are made of material which does not rot. Even nets which have broken away from ships continue to trap and kill sea life. When your family buys tins of tuna, check that the tin tells you that care was taken not to catch mammals like dolphins. If not, what can you do?

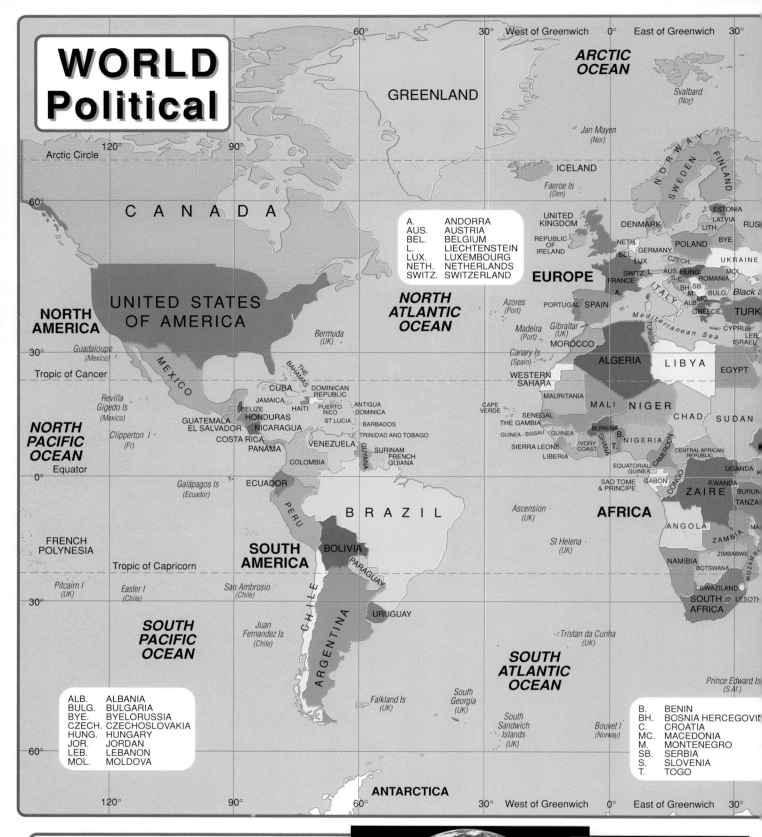

WORLD Political

ARCTIC OCEAN

GREENLAND

Svalbard *(Nor)*

Jan Mayen *(Nor)*

Arctic Circle

120°   90°   60°   30°   West of Greenwich   0°   East of Greenwich   30°

ICELAND

Faeroe Is *(Den)*

60°

C A N A D A

A.	ANDORRA
AUS.	AUSTRIA
BEL.	BELGIUM
L.	LIECHTENSTEIN
LUX.	LUXEMBOURG
NETH.	NETHERLANDS
SWITZ.	SWITZERLAND

UNITED KINGDOM

REPUBLIC OF IRELAND

NORWAY   SWEDEN   FINLAND

ESTONIA   LATVIA   LITH.   RUS.   BYE.

DENMARK   NETH.   GERMANY   POLAND   UKRAINE

BEL.   LUX.   CZECH.   AUS. HUNG.   MOL.   ROMANIA

SWITZ.   S.C.   BH.   M.   BULG.   Black

FRANCE   ITALY   ALB.   MC.   GREECE   TURK.

EUROPE

NORTH ATLANTIC OCEAN

UNITED STATES OF AMERICA

NORTH AMERICA

Azores *(Port)*

PORTUGAL   SPAIN

Madeira *(Port)*   Gibraltar *(UK)*   TUNISIA   Mediterranean Sea   CYPRUS   LEB.   ISRAEL

30°

Guadaloupe *(Mexico)*

Tropic of Cancer

Bermuda *(UK)*

Canary Is *(Spain)*   MOROCCO   ALGERIA   LIBYA   EGYPT

WESTERN SAHARA

MEXICO

Revilla Gigedo Is *(Mexico)*

THE BAHAMAS   CUBA   DOMINICAN REPUBLIC

MAURITANIA   MALI   NIGER   CHAD   SUDAN

CAPE VERDE

Clipperton I *(Fr)*

JAMAICA   BELIZE   HAITI   PUERTO RICO

ANTIGUA   DOMINICA   ST LUCIA   BARBADOS

SENEGAL   THE GAMBIA   BURKINA   B.   NIGERIA   CENTRAL AFRICAN REPUBLIC

GUATEMALA   HONDURAS   NICARAGUA

GUINEA - BISSAU   GUINEA   IVORY COAST   GHANA   CAMEROON

NORTH PACIFIC OCEAN

EL SALVADOR   COSTA RICA   PANAMA

TRINIDAD AND TOBAGO

SIERRA LEONE   LIBERIA

EQUATORIAL GUINEA

Equator

VENEZUELA   GUYANA   SURINAM   FRENCH GUIANA

SAO TOME & PRINCIPE   GABON   CONGO   ZAIRE   UGANDA   RWANDA   BURUN.   TANZA.

0°

COLOMBIA

Galápagos Is *(Ecuador)*   ECUADOR

AFRICA

Ascension *(UK)*

ANGOLA   ZAMBIA   MA.

PERU   B R A Z I L

FRENCH POLYNESIA

SOUTH AMERICA   BOLIVIA

St Helena *(UK)*

NAMIBIA   ZIMBABWE   MOZAM.

BOTSWANA

Tropic of Capricorn

PARAGUAY

SWAZILAND

Pitcairn I *(UK)*   Easter I *(Chile)*   San Ambrosio *(Chile)*

CHILE   URUGUAY

SOUTH AFRICA   LESOTH.

30°

Juan Fernandez Is *(Chile)*

SOUTH PACIFIC OCEAN

ARGENTINA

Tristan da Cunha *(UK)*

Prince Edward Is *(S.Af.)*

SOUTH ATLANTIC OCEAN

ALB.	ALBANIA
BULG.	BULGARIA
BYE.	BYELORUSSIA
CZECH.	CZECHOSLOVAKIA
HUNG.	HUNGARY
JOR.	JORDAN
LEB.	LEBANON
MOL.	MOLDOVA

Falkland Is *(UK)*

South Georgia *(UK)*

South Sandwich Islands *(UK)*

Bouvet I *(Norway)*

B.	BENIN
BH.	BOSNIA HERCEGOVI...
C.	CROATIA
MC.	MACEDONIA
M.	MONTENEGRO
SB.	SERBIA
S.	SLOVENIA
T.	TOGO

60°

120°   90°   60°   30°   West of Greenwich   0°   East of Greenwich   30°

ANTARCTICA

The Earth is a sphere. Satellite photographs give us a clear picture of the Earth in space. A globe provides a good model of the Earth, however it is not easy to carry a globe around or keep it in a bag! To provide information in an easy-to-read way the Earth needs to be shown on a flat map. The problem with turning a sphere into a map is that parts of the sphere need to be stretched to fit the paper.

34

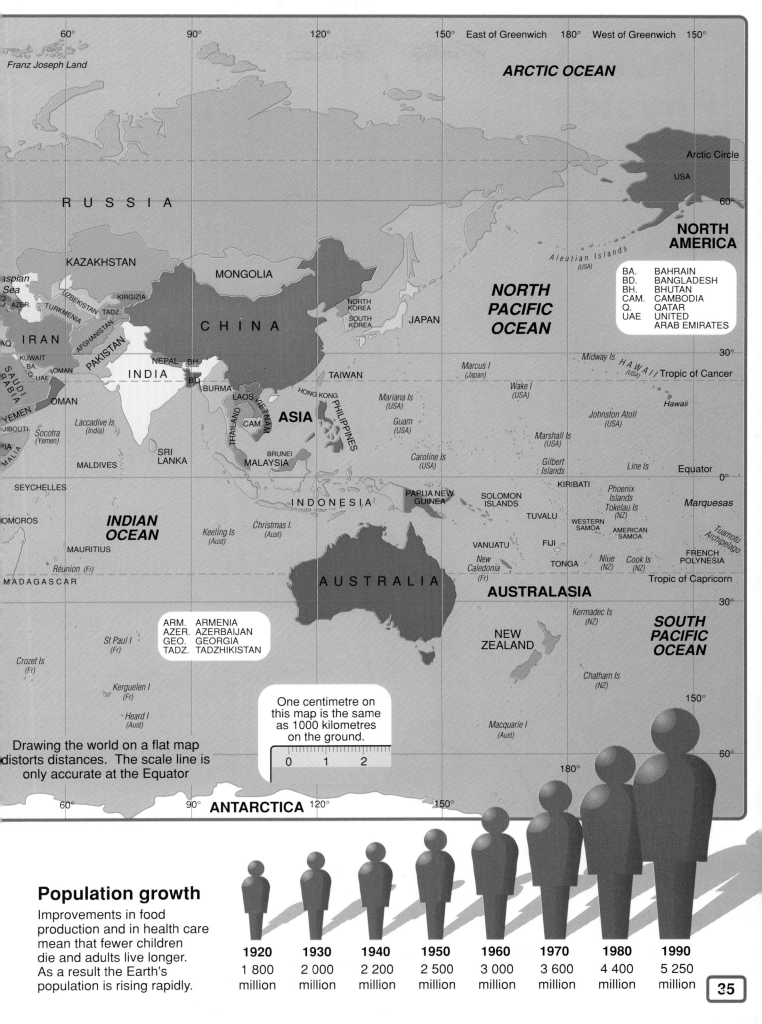

Franz Joseph Land

ARCTIC OCEAN

Arctic Circle

USA

60°

NORTH AMERICA

Aleutian Islands (USA)

R U S S I A

KAZAKHSTAN

MONGOLIA

aspian Sea

UZBEKISTAN
KIRGIZIA
. AZER. TURKMENIA TADZ.

C H I N A

NORTH KOREA

SOUTH KOREA

JAPAN

NORTH PACIFIC OCEAN

BA.	BAHRAIN
BD.	BANGLADESH
BH.	BHUTAN
CAM.	CAMBODIA
Q.	QATAR
UAE	UNITED ARAB EMIRATES

IRAN
AFGHANISTAN

AQ

KUWAIT
BA.
Q. UAE
OMAN

PAKISTAN

NEPAL BH.

INDIA   BD.

BURMA

Marcus I (Japan)

Wake I (USA)

Midway Is HAWAII (USA) Tropic of Cancer

30°

SAUDI ARABIA

YEMEN
JIBOUTI

OMAN

Laccadive Is (India)

Socotra (Yemen)

PIA
MALIA

TAIWAN

HONG KONG

LAOS VIETNAM
THAILAND
CAM.

PHILIPPINES

ASIA

Mariana Is (USA)

Guam (USA)

Johnston Atoll (USA)

Hawaii

SRI LANKA

MALAYSIA

BRUNEI

Caroline Is (USA)

Marshall Is (USA)

Gilbert Islands

Line Is

Equator 0°

MALDIVES

SEYCHELLES

I N D O N E S I A

PAPUA NEW GUINEA

SOLOMON ISLANDS

KIRIBATI

Phoenix Islands
Tokelau Is (NZ)

Marquesas

OMOROS

INDIAN OCEAN

MAURITIUS

Réunion (Fr)

Keeling Is (Aust)

Christmas I. (Aust)

TUVALU

WESTERN SAMOA

AMERICAN SAMOA

Tuamotu Archipelago

MADAGASCAR

VANUATU

FIJI

New Caledonia (Fr)

TONGA

Niue (NZ)

Cook Is (NZ)

FRENCH POLYNESIA

A U S T R A L I A

AUSTRALASIA

Tropic of Capricorn

30°

ARM.	ARMENIA
AZER.	AZERBAIJAN
GEO.	GEORGIA
TADZ.	TADZHIKISTAN

St Paul I (Fr)

Crozet Is (Fr)

Kerguelen I (Fr)

Heard I (Aust)

One centimetre on this map is the same as 1000 kilometres on the ground.

0 1 2

Kermadec Is (NZ)

NEW ZEALAND

Chatham Is (NZ)

SOUTH PACIFIC OCEAN

150°

Drawing the world on a flat map distorts distances. The scale line is only accurate at the Equator

Macquarie I (Aust)

60°

60°   90° **ANTARCTICA** 120°   150°

180°

Population growth

Improvements in food production and in health care mean that fewer children die and adults live longer. As a result the Earth's population is rising rapidly.

1920	1930	1940	1950	1960	1970	1980	1990
1 800 million	2 000 million	2 200 million	2 500 million	3 000 million	3 600 million	4 400 million	5 250 million

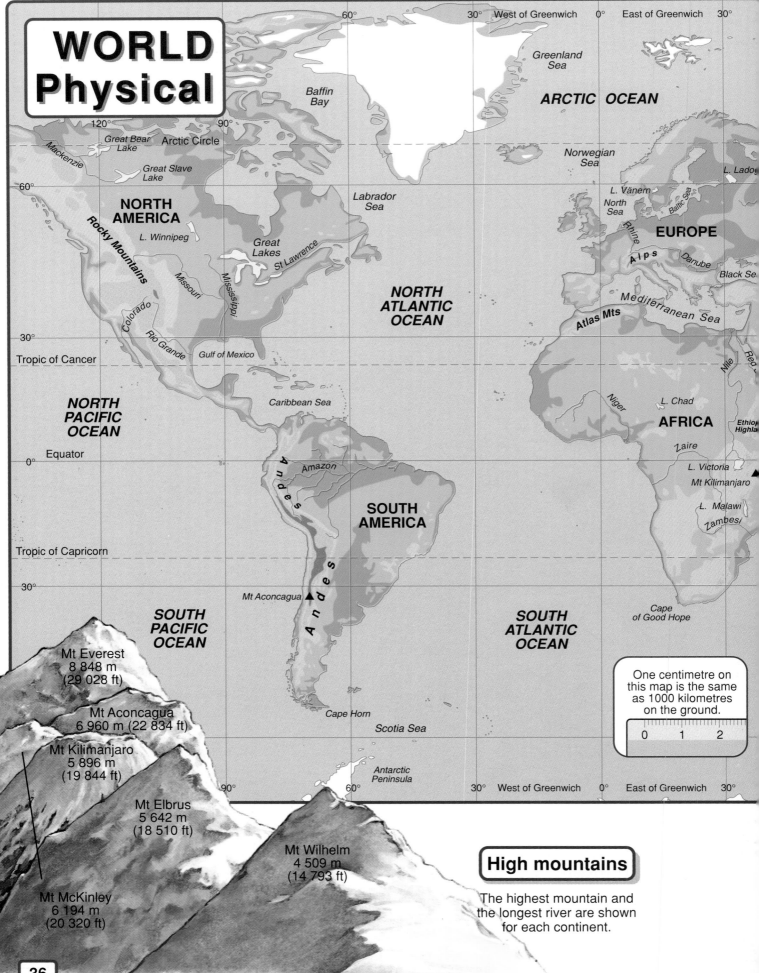

WORLD Physical

ARCTIC OCEAN

Greenland Sea

Baffin Bay

Arctic Circle

Mackenzie

Great Bear Lake

Great Slave Lake

Norwegian Sea

L. Ladoga

60°

NORTH AMERICA

Rocky Mountains

L. Winnipeg

Labrador Sea

Great Lakes

St Lawrence

Missouri

Mississippi

L. Vänern

North Sea

Baltic Sea

EUROPE

Rhine

Alps

Danube

Black Sea

NORTH ATLANTIC OCEAN

Mediterranean Sea

Atlas Mts

30°

Tropic of Cancer

Colorado

Rio Grande

Gulf of Mexico

Niger

Nile

Red Sea

L. Chad

AFRICA

Ethiop. Highla.

NORTH PACIFIC OCEAN

Caribbean Sea

Zaire

L. Victoria

Mt Kilimanjaro

0°   Equator

Andes

Amazon

SOUTH AMERICA

L. Malawi

Zambesi

Tropic of Capricorn

Andes

Mt Aconcagua

SOUTH PACIFIC OCEAN

SOUTH ATLANTIC OCEAN

Cape of Good Hope

30°

Mt Everest
8 848 m
(29 028 ft)

Mt Aconcagua
6 960 m (22 834 ft)

Mt Kilimanjaro
5 896 m
(19 844 ft)

Cape Horn

Scotia Sea

One centimetre on this map is the same as 1000 kilometres on the ground.

0   1   2

Mt Elbrus
5 642 m
(18 510 ft)

Antarctic Peninsula

Mt Wilhelm
4 509 m
(14 793 ft)

High mountains

Mt McKinley
6 194 m
(20 320 ft)

The highest mountain and the longest river are shown for each continent.

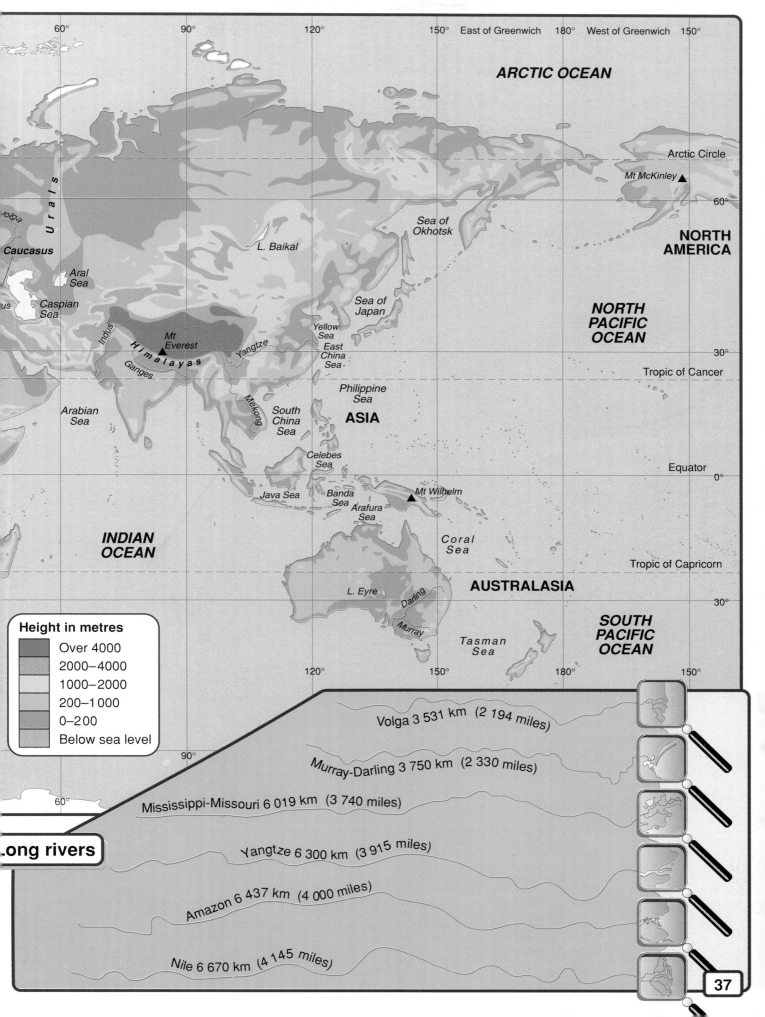

ARCTIC OCEAN

Arctic Circle

Mt McKinley ▲

60°

NORTH
AMERICA

NORTH
PACIFIC
OCEAN

30°

Tropic of Cancer

Equator 0°

Tropic of Capricorn

30°

SOUTH
PACIFIC
OCEAN

U r a l s

Volga

Caucasus

*Aral
Sea*

*Caspian
Sea*

us

Indus

Ganges

H i m a l a y a s

Mt
Everest ▲

Yangtze

Mekong

L. Baikal

Sea of
Okhotsk

Sea of
Japan

Yellow
Sea

East
China
Sea

Philippine
Sea

ASIA

*Arabian
Sea*

*South
China
Sea*

Celebes
Sea

Java Sea

Banda
Sea

Arafura
Sea

Mt Wilhelm ▲

Coral
Sea

INDIAN
OCEAN

AUSTRALASIA

L. Eyre

Darling

Murray

Tasman
Sea

Height in metres

	Over 4000
	2000–4000
	1000–2000
	200–1 000
	0–200
	Below sea level

ong rivers

Volga 3 531 km (2 194 miles)

Murray-Darling 3 750 km (2 330 miles)

Mississippi-Missouri 6 019 km (3 740 miles)

Yangtze 6 300 km (3 915 miles)

Amazon 6 437 km (4 000 miles)

Nile 6 670 km (4 145 miles)

60°

EUROPE Political

Population

10 million people

Continental population is 700 million.

European former Soviet Republics 190 million

Germany 78 m

United Kingdom 57 m

France 57 m

Poland 38 m

Norway 4.5 m

Liechtenstein 28 000

Main languages spoken

English German French

Italian Russian Spanish

Most European countries have their own language.

Life expectancy

= 10 years

70 Hungary
73 Italy
69 Portugal
76 Sweden
71 UK

Religion

The majority of Europeans are Christian. There is also a large number of atheists and a growing number of Muslims

Capital city
Other town

One centimetre on this map is the same as 400 kilometres on the ground.

0 1 2

Republics of Czechoslovakia
CL. THE CZECH LANDS
S.   SLOVAKIA

Countries formerly Yugoslavia
AND.   ANDORRA   LIECHTENSTEIN
L.   LUXEMBOURG
LUX.   LUXEMBOURG
SWITZ. SWITZERLAND

BH.   BOSNIA HERCEGOVINA
CR.   CROATIA
MC.   MACEDONIA
MN.   MONTENEGRO
SR.   SERBIA

ARCTIC OCEAN

NORTH ATLANTIC OCEAN

Arctic Circle

ICELAND
● Reykjavik

Faeroe Is (Dmk)

UNITED KINGDOM
REPUBLIC OF IRELAND
Dublin
London

NETHER-LANDS
Amsterdam
BELGIUM
Brussels
LUX.
Paris ◉
FRANCE

PORTUGAL
Lisbon ◉
SPAIN
Madrid ◉
Gibraltar ●
AFRICA

North Sea

Bergen ●

N O R W A Y
Oslo ◉
S W E D E N
Stockholm ◉
DENMARK
Copenhagen ◉

F I N L A N D
Kuusamo ●
Helsinki ◉

GERMANY
Berlin ◉
Bern ◉
SWITZ.
AND.

CZECHOSLOVAKIA
Prague ◉ CL.
Viennna ◉ S.
AUSTRIA
Ljubljana ◉
SL.
Zagreb ◉
CR.
Sarajevo ◉
BH.
Podgorica ◉
MN.
Tirana ◉
ALBANIA

POLAND
Warsaw ◉

HUNGARY
Budapest ◉
Bratislava ◉

Belgrade ◉
SB.
Skopje ◉
MC.

I T A L Y
Rome ◉

Tallinn ◉ ESTONIA
Riga ◉ LATVIA
LITHUANIA
Vilnius ◉
RUSSIA
Minsk ◉
BYELORUSSIA

Kiev ◉
U K R A I N E
Kishinev ◉
MOLDOVA

ROMANIA
Bucharest ◉
BULGARIA
Sofia ◉

GREECE
Athens ◉
Iraklion ●
Crete ●

Mediterranean

Black Sea

TURKEY

R U S S I A
Moscow ◉

Caspian Sea

GEORGIA
Tbilisi ◉
ARMENIA
Yerevan ◉
AZERBAIJAN
Baku ◉

ASIA

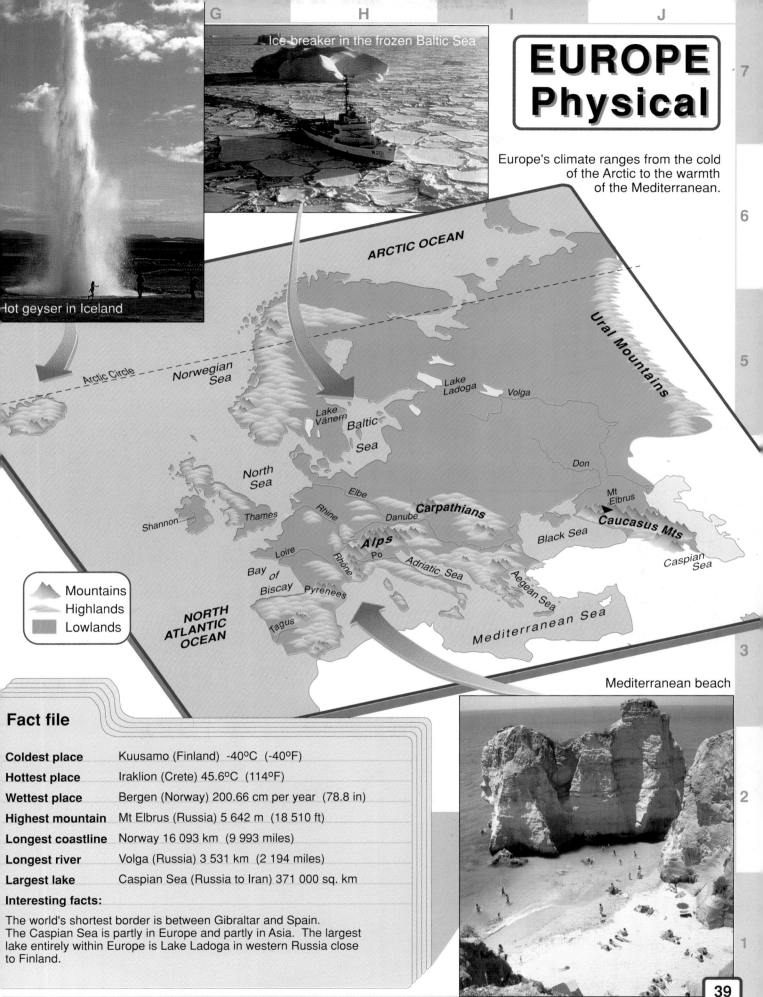

Ice-breaker in the frozen Baltic Sea

Hot geyser in Iceland

EUROPE Physical

Europe's climate ranges from the cold of the Arctic to the warmth of the Mediterranean.

ARCTIC OCEAN

Ural Mountains

Arctic Circle

Norwegian Sea

Lake Ladoga

Volga

Lake Vänern

Baltic Sea

North Sea

Don

Elbe

Mt Elbrus

Shannon

Thames

Rhine

Danube

Carpathians

Caucasus Mts

Black Sea

Alps

Po

Caspian Sea

Loire

Rhône

Adriatic Sea

Bay of Biscay

Pyrenees

Aegean Sea

Mountains
Highlands
Lowlands

NORTH ATLANTIC OCEAN

Tagus

Mediterranean Sea

Mediterranean beach

Fact file

Coldest place	Kuusamo (Finland) -40°C (-40°F)
Hottest place	Iraklion (Crete) 45.6°C (114°F)
Wettest place	Bergen (Norway) 200.66 cm per year (78.8 in)
Highest mountain	Mt Elbrus (Russia) 5 642 m (18 510 ft)
Longest coastline	Norway 16 093 km (9 993 miles)
Longest river	Volga (Russia) 3 531 km (2 194 miles)
Largest lake	Caspian Sea (Russia to Iran) 371 000 sq. km

Interesting facts:

The world's shortest border is between Gibraltar and Spain. The Caspian Sea is partly in Europe and partly in Asia. The largest lake entirely within Europe is Lake Ladoga in western Russia close to Finland.

EUROPE Global Issues

Acid rain

Acid rain is formed when pollution from power stations, factories and vehicles rises into the air and mixes with raindrops. The wind blows the rainclouds. The acid rain often falls far away from the area where the pollution was created. Acid rain affects streams and lakes. Many become so polluted that fish life is completely destroyed. Forests too are being badly damaged by acid rain. In Europe the polluted air is blown by the SW winds and causes damage in northern Europe and Scandinavia.

Arctic Circle

Areas causing high pollution

South west wind

Before

15 years later

Industrial pollution

Polluted clouds

Environmental damage

Acid rain

Fish killed by pollution

Gasping for air

Crisis in Athens

During the summer the air in Athens can be so bad that people die. Athens has grown rapidly this century. Millions of people have moved there. On a hot day fumes from factories and from the large number of old cars stuck in the traffic jams poison the air. If there is no wind to blow the foul air away it simply gets worse and worse. This not only affects the people. Many of the magnificent ancient buildings of Athens are being damaged by air pollution.

When conditions are really bad the Mayor of Athens has to take emergency action. Sometimes only cars with four passengers are allowed into the city. There are even days when all cars have been banned from Athens. Other cities around the world have the same problem. In many of them masks are worn to reduce the effects of the poisonous air.

G R E E C E

Athens

Piraeus

Athens

Parthenon, Athens

As people in the rich world grow richer many families own two or three cars. As standards of living improve in the economically developing world more and more cars will be bought and driven. What other types of transport will need to be available in large cities if people are to leave their cars at home?

World of cars

The picture shows the number of cars compared with the size of the population. For example, for every 100 people in the USA there are more than 50 cars; in China there is fewer than 1 car for every 100 people.

50% +
USA

30% +
Canada Australia
Sweden France

10% +
UK
Japan
Spain
Greece

5% +
Brazil
South
Africa
Saudi
Arabia

1%-5%
Russia
Peru
Morocco

<1%
China
India
Zaire

ASIA Political

The variety of languages, cultures, dress, diet, homes and lifestyles is enormous. The old and new exist side by side. Many different alphabets are in use across Asia.

Main languages spoken

Farsi · Russian · French · Turkish · Arabic · Japanese · English · Hindi · Mandarin

Capital city ◉
Other city ●

One centimetre on this map is the same as 750 kilometres on the ground.

0   1   2

Life expectancy

☐ = 10 years

75 — Japan
60 — Turkey
48 — S. Arabia
47 — Bangladesh
44 — Laos

Population

Asia contains the countries with the world's highest populations. China already has more than 1 000 million people. India too will reach 1 000 million by the year 2000.

= 100 million people
= 10 million people

Continental population is 3 000 million.

China 1 100 million
India 850 m
Indonesia 180 m
Pakistan 110 m
Cambodia 6 m
Singapore 2.5 m
Mongolia 2 m

Religion

Area	Main belief
From Turkey to Pakistan	Islam
India	Hinduism
SE Asia	Buddhism
Indonesia	Islam
Philippines	Christianity

All of the world's major

Map labels

ARCTIC OCEAN

RUSSIA
• Yakutsk
• Moscow

Arctic Circle

EUROPE

KAZAKHSTAN
Alma Ata
Frunze
KIRGIZIA
Tashkent
UZBEKISTAN
TADZHIKISTAN
Dushanbe
TURKMENIA
Ashkhabad
Kabul
AFGHANISTAN
Islamabad
PAKISTAN
New Delhi
INDIA

MONGOLIA
Ulan Bator

C H I N A
Beijing

NORTH KOREA
Pyongyang
SOUTH KOREA
Seoul
Vladivostok
JAPAN
Tokyo

NEPAL
Kathmandu
Thimphu
BHUTAN
Cherrapunji
BANGLADESH
Dhaka
BURMA
Rangoon
Vientiane
LAOS
THAILAND
Bangkok
Hanoi
VIETNAM
CAMBODIA
Phnom Penh

TAIWAN
Taipei
HONG KONG (UK)
PHILIPPINES
Manila

MALAYSIA
Kuala Lumpur
Singapore
BRUNEI
Bandar Seri Begawan
INDONESIA
Jakarta

SRI LANKA
Colombo

Tropic of Cancer
Equator

INDIAN OCEAN
NORTH PACIFIC OCEAN

TURKEY
Ankara
Nicosia
CYPRUS
LEBANON
Tel Aviv
ISRAEL
SYRIA
Damascus
Amman
JORDAN
IRAQ
Baghdad
Tehran
I R A N
KUWAIT
Kuwait
Abadan
BAHRAIN
QATAR
Doha
Riyadh
SAUDI ARABIA
UNITED ARAB EMIRATES
Abu Dhabi
Muscat
OMAN
YEMEN
San'a

AFRICA

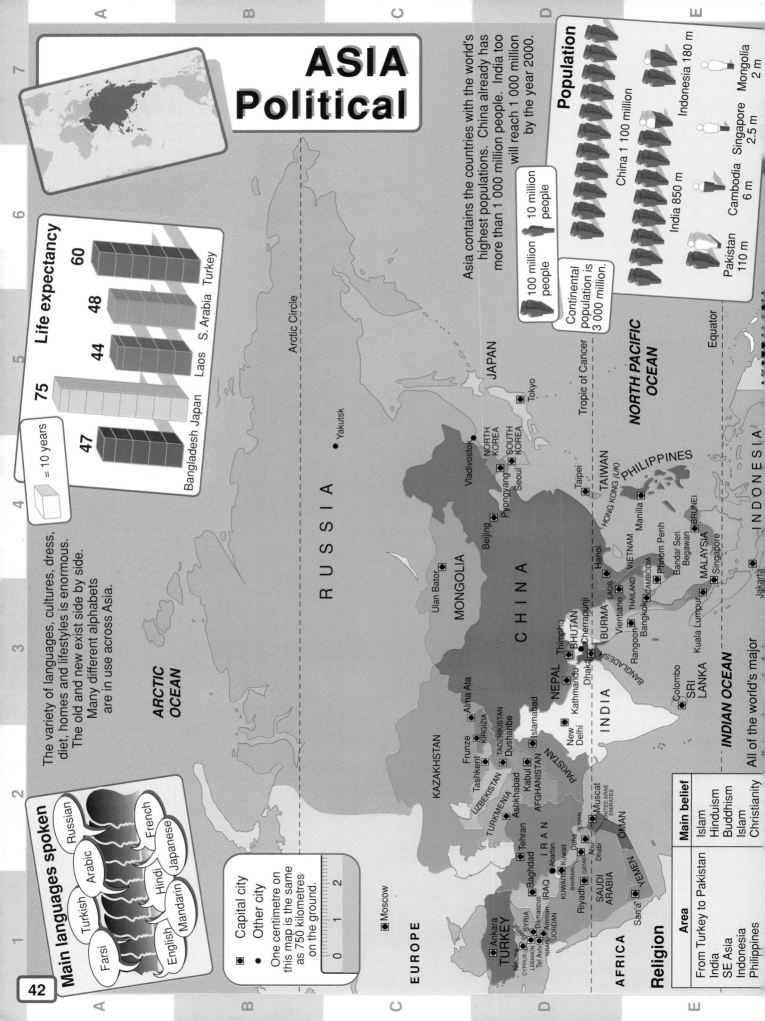

The climates of Asia range from the extreme cold of Arctic Russia to the intense heat of equatorial Indonesia.

Taiga

Arabian Desert

ARCTIC OCEAN

Ural Mts

Siberia

Arctic Circle

Steppes

Aral Sea

Caspian Sea

Lake Baikal

Tian Shan

Altai

Gobi Desert

Arabian Desert

Persian Gulf

Indus

Himalayas

Mt Everest

Ganges

Brahmaputra

Yangtze

Sea of Japan

Arabian Sea

Bay of Bengal

Mekong

NORTH PACIFIC OCEAN

INDIAN OCEAN

South China Sea

Philippine Sea

Tropic of Cancer

Sumatera

Borneo

Equator

Mountains
Highlands
Lowlands
Deserts

Fact file

Coldest place	Yakutsk (Russia) -64.3ºC (-84ºF)
Hottest place	Abadan (Iran) 52.8ºC (127ºF)
Wettest place	Cherrapunji (India) 1 079.5 cm per year (425.1 in)
Highest mountain	Mt Everest (Nepal/China) 8 848 m (29 028 ft)
Longest coastline	Indonesia 54 716 km (33 978 miles)
Longest river	Yangtze [Chang Jiang] (China) 6 300 km (3 915 miles)
Largest lake	Caspian Sea (Russia to Iran) 371 000 sq. km (143 205 sq. miles)

Interesting facts:

Asia is the world's largest continent; it covers almost one third of the world's land surface.
60% of the world's population live in Asia.
The world's longest railway is the Trans-Siberian which is 9 438 km (5 864 miles) long and links Moscow with Vladivostok.

Mount Everest

ASIA Global Issues

Population growth

The growth of the world's population leads to an increased demand on food and other resources. Europe had its rapid population growth in the last century. Today growth is greatest in Asia, Africa, Central and South America.

The problem

Housing and feeding a growing population is not easy. Different countries try different methods of dealing with this challenge.

China: The response

In China people are not allowed to move from the countryside to the city without permission. This is to avoid large numbers of homeless people living in shanty towns. Parents in most of China are expected to have only one child.

Indonesia: The response

Indonesia is a country of many islands. Peo[ple] from the main islands such as Jawa are giv[en] land in other parts of Indone[sia] including Timor a[nd] Irian Ja[ya]

CHINA

Tropic of Cancer

Equator

INDONESIA *Irian Jaya*

Jawa

Timor

One problem now facing China is that of spoilt children. Grandparents, parents and relatives give so much time and attention to the only child that many now have the nickname 'The Little Emperor'.

'Freedom fighters' - East Timor

The native people of Timor and Irian Jaya have seen their forests destroyed to provid[e] land for the new settlers. Today many natives, whos[e] families have lived there fo[r] generations, are fighting th[e] Indonesian government an[d] demanding independence and an end to the settlements.

44

Monsoon areas of the world

As summer comes to monsoon areas the land warms up. The air above it rises and fresh air is drawn from over the ocean. This air is heavy with water which has evaporated from the sea. Clouds travel and pass over the land where they drop enormous quantities of rain. In South Asia the wind carries moisture from the Indian Ocean to the surrounding land.

Many parts of the world around the tropics depend on heavy rain for the crops to grow. This rain is *seasonal* and is known as the *Monsoon*. The monsoon should mean good news for the farmers but sometimes it means disaster.

Natural disasters

A hurricane develops

Sometimes the monsoon can turn into a hurricane. A hurricane spins as it crosses the ocean. It collects more and more rain as it travels. Hurricane force winds develop. Giant waves are formed. They can destroy everything on low lying land.

Water evaporates from the ocean.

Sun's rays

Rain clouds form; winds strengthen over the ocean.

Rain clouds and strong winds spiral towards the land. Giant waves form.

INDIA

BANGLADESH

Tropic of Cancer

Dhaka

• Chittagong

BURMA

INDIA

Cox's Bazar •

Bay of Bengal

INDIAN OCEAN

Bangladesh is in the path of such hurricanes. The coast is very low, flat and exposed. When the hurricane arrives it can destroy everything in its path.

Effect of the 1991 hurricane on Bangladesh.

45

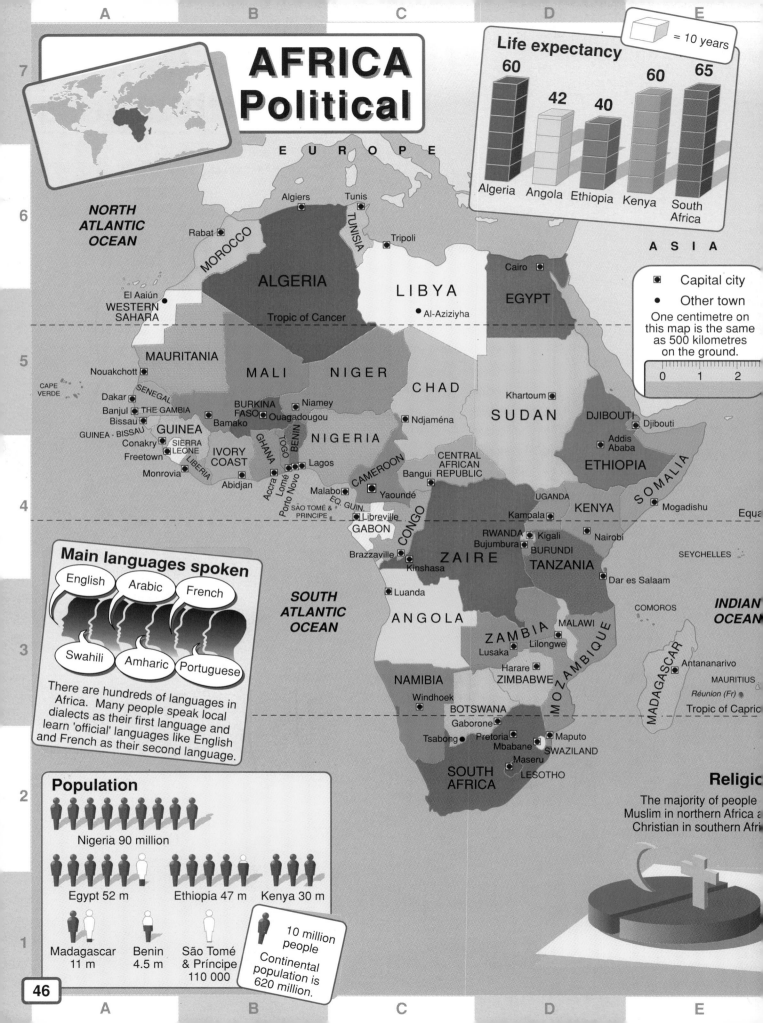

AFRICA Political

Life expectancy ☐ = 10 years

Algeria	Angola	Ethiopia	Kenya	South Africa
60	42	40	60	65

- ◉ Capital city
- ● Other town

One centimetre on this map is the same as 500 kilometres on the ground.

0   1   2

EUROPE

ASIA

NORTH ATLANTIC OCEAN

SOUTH ATLANTIC OCEAN

INDIAN OCEAN

Tropic of Cancer

Tropic of Capric

Equa

Countries and places:
MOROCCO — Rabat, Algiers
TUNISIA — Tunis, Tripoli
ALGERIA
LIBYA — Al-Aziziyha
EGYPT — Cairo
WESTERN SAHARA — El Aaiún
MAURITANIA — Nouakchott
MALI — Bamako
NIGER — Niamey
CHAD — Ndjaména
SUDAN — Khartoum
CAPE VERDE
SENEGAL — Dakar
THE GAMBIA — Banjul
GUINEA - BISSAU — Bissau
GUINEA — Conakry
SIERRA LEONE — Freetown
LIBERIA — Monrovia
IVORY COAST — Abidjan
BURKINA FASO — Ouagadougou
GHANA — Accra
TOGO — Lomé
BENIN — Porto Novo
NIGERIA — Lagos
SÃO TOMÉ & PRÍNCIPE
EQ. GUIN. — Malabo
CAMEROON — Yaoundé
CENTRAL AFRICAN REPUBLIC — Bangui
GABON — Libreville
CONGO — Brazzaville
ZAIRE — Kinshasa
UGANDA — Kampala
RWANDA — Kigali
BURUNDI — Bujumbura
KENYA — Nairobi
TANZANIA — Dar es Salaam
SOMALIA — Mogadishu
DJIBOUTI — Djibouti
ETHIOPIA — Addis Ababa
SEYCHELLES
COMOROS
ANGOLA — Luanda
ZAMBIA — Lusaka
MALAWI — Lilongwe
MOZAMBIQUE — Maputo
ZIMBABWE — Harare
NAMIBIA — Windhoek
BOTSWANA — Gaborone, Tsabong
MADAGASCAR — Antananarivo
MAURITIUS
Réunion (Fr)
SOUTH AFRICA — Pretoria
SWAZILAND — Mbabane
LESOTHO — Maseru

Main languages spoken

English   Arabic   French
Swahili   Amharic   Portuguese

There are hundreds of languages in Africa. Many people speak local dialects as their first language and learn 'official' languages like English and French as their second language.

Population

Nigeria 90 million
Egypt 52 m
Ethiopia 47 m
Kenya 30 m
Madagascar 11 m
Benin 4.5 m
São Tomé & Príncipe 110 000

☻ 10 million people
Continental population is 620 million.

Religio

The majority of people
Muslim in northern Africa a
Christian in southern Afri

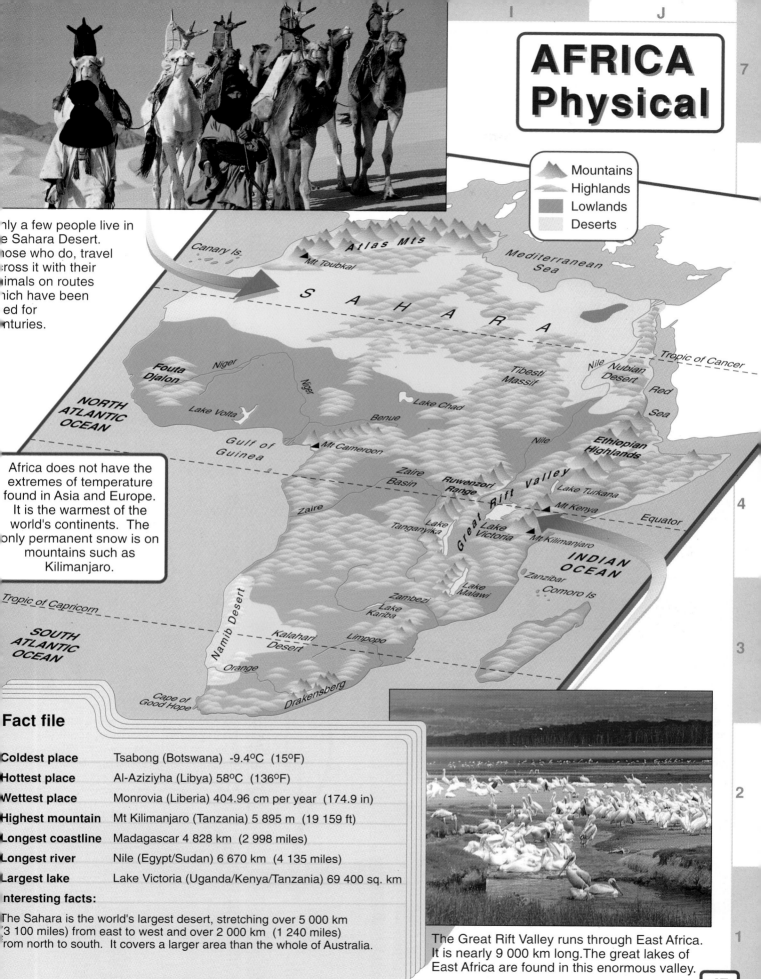

nly a few people live in e Sahara Desert. ose who do, travel ross it with their imals on routes ich have been ed for nturies.

Africa does not have the extremes of temperature found in Asia and Europe. It is the warmest of the world's continents. The only permanent snow is on mountains such as Kilimanjaro.

Legend:
- Mountains
- Highlands
- Lowlands
- Deserts

Map labels:
Canary Is., Atlas Mts, Mt Toubkal, Mediterranean Sea, SAHARA, Tropic of Cancer, Fouta Djalon, Niger, Niger, Tibesti Massif, Nile, Nubian Desert, Red Sea, NORTH ATLANTIC OCEAN, Lake Volta, Lake Chad, Benue, Gulf of Guinea, Mt Cameroon, Nile, Ethiopian Highlands, Zaire Basin, Ruwenzori Range, Great Rift Valley, Lake Turkana, Zaire, Mt Kenya, Equator, Lake Tanganyika, Lake Victoria, Mt Kilimanjaro, INDIAN OCEAN, Zanzibar, Comoro Is, Lake Malawi, Zambezi, Lake Kariba, Namib Desert, Tropic of Capricorn, SOUTH ATLANTIC OCEAN, Kalahari Desert, Limpopo, Orange, Cape of Good Hope, Drakensberg

Fact file

Coldest place	Tsabong (Botswana) -9.4°C (15°F)
Hottest place	Al-Aziziyha (Libya) 58°C (136°F)
Wettest place	Monrovia (Liberia) 404.96 cm per year (174.9 in)
Highest mountain	Mt Kilimanjaro (Tanzania) 5 895 m (19 159 ft)
Longest coastline	Madagascar 4 828 km (2 998 miles)
Longest river	Nile (Egypt/Sudan) 6 670 km (4 135 miles)
Largest lake	Lake Victoria (Uganda/Kenya/Tanzania) 69 400 sq. km

Interesting facts:

The Sahara is the world's largest desert, stretching over 5 000 km (3 100 miles) from east to west and over 2 000 km (1 240 miles) from north to south. It covers a larger area than the whole of Australia.

The Great Rift Valley runs through East Africa. It is nearly 9 000 km long. The great lakes of East Africa are found in this enormous valley.

AFRICA Global Issues

Around the world, wildlife is under threat. Some species have already disappeared forever. Others are in danger now.

The world elephant population

Elephants in Africa

- In the past
- Today

Tropic of Cancer

Equator

Tropic of Capricorn

In Africa the elephant population has been shrinking rapidly. There are three main reasons:

1 More and more of the land is used by people for farming. The elephants' habitat is therefore being destroyed.
2 Elephants have been killed for their ivory which can be sold for large amounts of money.
3 Changes in the climate.

Some countries have protected the elephants by providing nature reserves, where elephant numbers are controlled but elephants can enjoy a natural existence. The nature reserves attract tourists who bring much needed money to the area.

Goods carved from ivory were once sold all around the world. Now most countries have agreed to ban the trade in ivory. When ivory is taken from poachers it is burned. This is to prevent the trade continuing.

20 years ago	3 000 000 elephants
10 years ago	1 300 000
Today	600 000
?	The last elephant?

What should anyone who cares about the future of elephants do if offered the chance to buy ivory products?

Deserts of the World

The area of the world covered by desert is increasing.

Advancing deserts

The rains which used to come regularly to Ethiopia and Sudan are no longer reliable. Without the rain, crops do not grow and the natural vegetation on which animals live is also damaged.

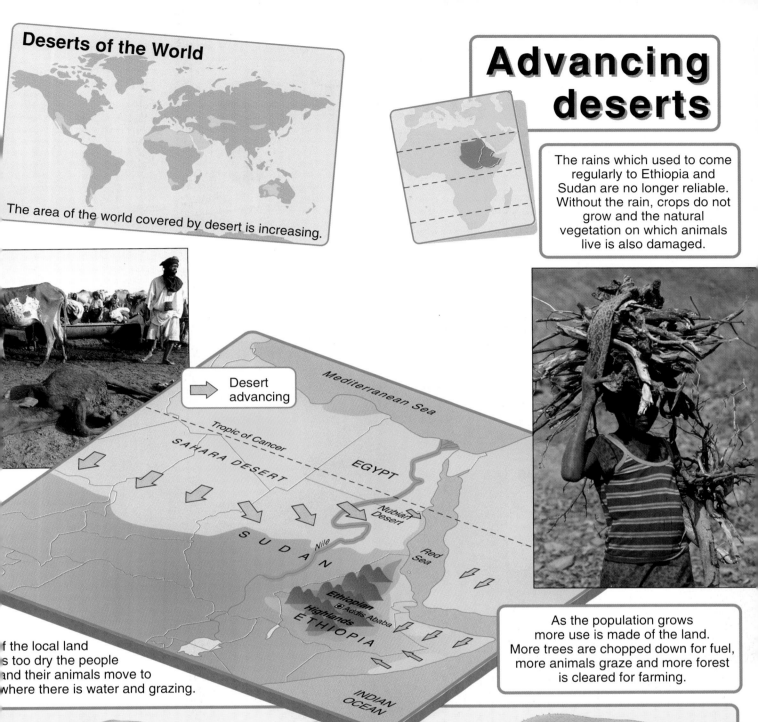

Desert advancing

Mediterranean Sea

Tropic of Cancer

SAHARA DESERT

EGYPT

Nubian Desert

S U D A N

Nile

Red Sea

Ethiopian Highlands
Addis Ababa
E T H I O P I A

INDIAN OCEAN

f the local land
s too dry the people
and their animals move to
where there is water and grazing.

As the population grows more use is made of the land. More trees are chopped down for fuel, more animals graze and more forest is cleared for farming.

The extra animals eat the young trees before they can grow.

Without the trees the soil becomes loose.

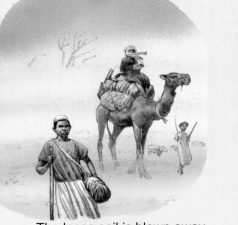

The loose soil is blown away, fewer crops grow and the land turns to desert.

SOUTH AMERICA Political

Life expectancy

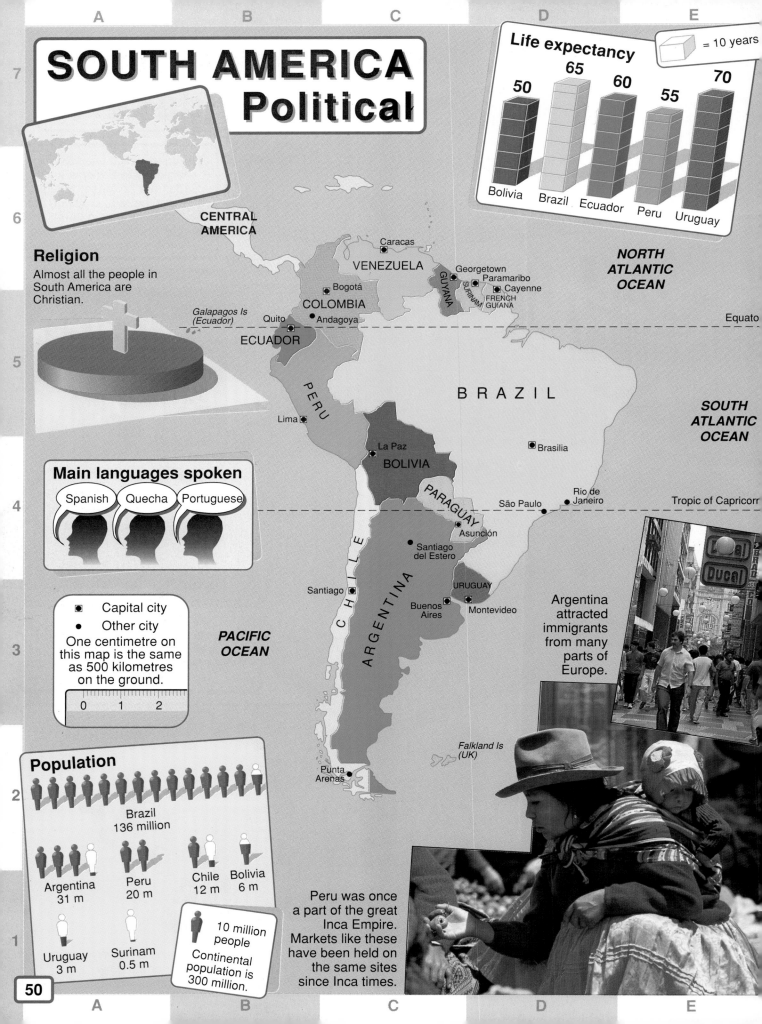

= 10 years

50 Bolivia
65 Brazil
60 Ecuador
55 Peru
70 Uruguay

Religion

Almost all the people in South America are Christian.

Main languages spoken

Spanish   Quecha   Portuguese

Capital city
Other city
One centimetre on this map is the same as 500 kilometres on the ground.

0   1   2

Population

Brazil 136 million

Argentina 31 m
Peru 20 m
Chile 12 m
Bolivia 6 m

Uruguay 3 m
Surinam 0.5 m

10 million people
Continental population is 300 million.

CENTRAL AMERICA

Caracas
VENEZUELA
Georgetown
Paramaribo
Cayenne
GUYANA
SURINAM
FRENCH GUIANA
Bogotá
COLOMBIA
Galapagos Is (Ecuador)
Quito
Andagoya
ECUADOR
Equato
PERU
Lima
BRAZIL
La Paz
BOLIVIA
Brasilia
PARAGUAY
São Paulo
Rio de Janeiro
Tropic of Capricorr
Asunción
Santiago del Estero
CHILE
ARGENTINA
URUGUAY
Santiago
Buenos Aires
Montevideo
PACIFIC OCEAN
Falkland Is (UK)
Punta Arenas

NORTH ATLANTIC OCEAN

SOUTH ATLANTIC OCEAN

Argentina attracted immigrants from many parts of Europe.

Peru was once a part of the great Inca Empire. Markets like these have been held on the same sites since Inca times.

Amazon River

SOUTH AMERICA
Physical

Equator

Orinoco

Angel Falls

Amazon

Amazon Basin

Paraná

Andes

L. Titicaca

Paraguay

Atacama
Desert

Tropic of
Capricorn

Andes

Aconcagua ▲

Pampas

River
Plate

Amazon
Rainforest

SOUTH
ATLANTIC
OCEAN

SOUTH
PACIFIC
OCEAN

Cape Horn

Andes

	Mountains
	Highlands
	Lowlands
	Deserts

Fact file

Coldest place	Punta Arenas (Chile) -11.7 °C (11 °F)
Hottest place	Santiago del Estero (Argentina) 46.7 °C (116 °F)
Wettest place	Andagoya (Colombia) 713.74 cm per year (281.1 in)
Highest mountain	Aconcagua (Argentina) 6 960 m (22 834 ft)
Longest coastline	Brazil 7 491 km (4 652 miles)
Longest river	Amazon (Brazil/Peru) 6 437 km (4 000 miles)
Largest lake	Lake Titicaca (Bolivia/Peru) 8 285 sq. km (3 200 sq. miles)

Interesting facts:

Lake Titicaca is the highest lake with ships on it in the world. It is 3 811 metres (12 506 ft) above sea level.

There was no rainfall in the Atacama Desert for over 400 years.

Atacama Desert

SOUTH AMERICA
Global Issues

Tropical rainforests of the world

The high temperatures and heavy rainfall in lowland areas around the Equator provide perfect conditions for the growth of rainforests

Legend:
- Rainforest
- Mountains
- River

One centimetre on this map is the same as 500 kilometres on the ground.

0   1   2

Orinoco

Cotopaxi
Chimborazo

Amazon   *Amazon*

Equator

A n d e s

Paraguay   *Paraná*

Tropic of Capricorn

A n d e s

▲ *Aconcagua*

Yes, we cut the trees down and burn the stumps to clear the land. We farm it for 2 years then move on and the forest grows again.

Every day the world loses an area of rainforest equal to 300 000 soccer pitches. Where will it end?

I clear the forest and sell the wood. The land can be used to grow food for our city people. This provides jobs for farmers. It's not my problem that the land will be ruined; anyway there's lots more.

Value of the rainforests

Helps keep the world climate in balance. The rainforest soaks up the heavy rainfall, some which slowly joins the rivers, and the rest evaporates, ready to fall again

Home for traditional peoples

Wood products

Rosy periwinkle is used in drugs to treat leukaemia

Home for millions of species of animal, insect and plant life

Many new drugs are developed from rainforest plants

The world's rainforests are disappearing fast. Governments know this but they also need the money that comes from selling hardwood, the land for people to farm, and food for the towns and cities.

City growth

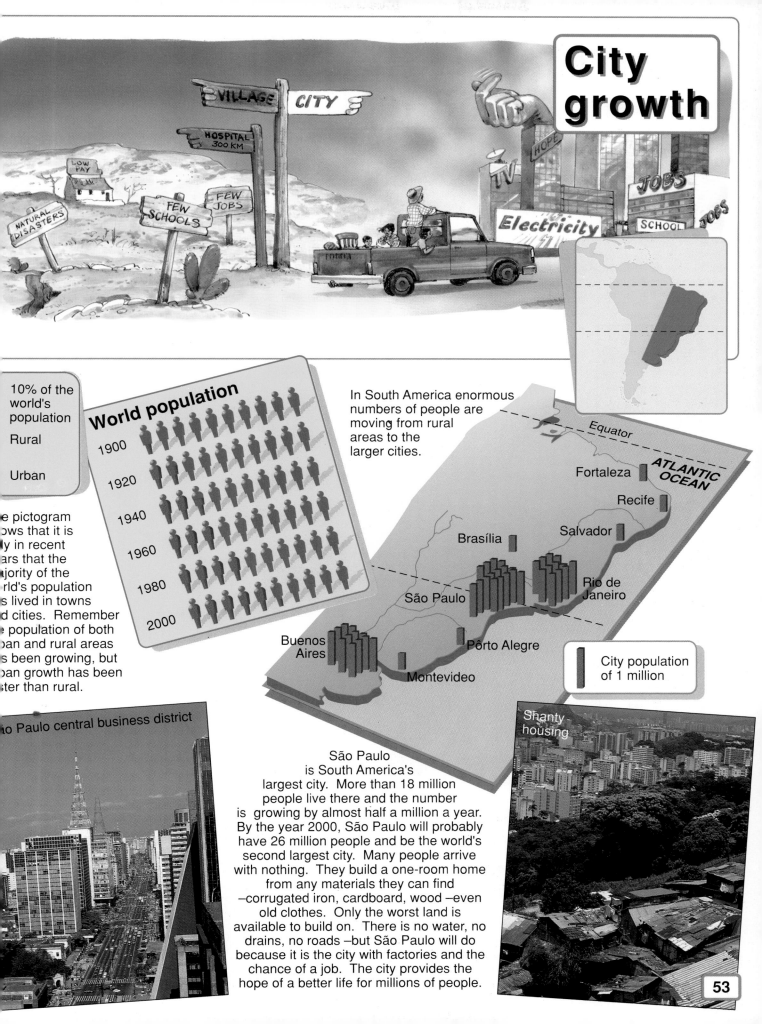

10% of the world's population

Rural

Urban

e pictogram
ows that it is
ly in recent
ars that the
ajority of the
rld's population
s lived in towns
d cities. Remember
e population of both
ban and rural areas
s been growing, but
ban growth has been
ster than rural.

World population

1900
1920
1940
1960
1980
2000

In South America enormous numbers of people are moving from rural areas to the larger cities.

Equator

ATLANTIC OCEAN

Fortaleza

Recife

Salvador

Brasília

Rio de Janeiro

São Paulo

Buenos Aires

Pôrto Alegre

Montevideo

City population of 1 million

o Paulo central business district

Shanty housing

São Paulo
is South America's
largest city. More than 18 million
people live there and the number
is growing by almost half a million a year.
By the year 2000, São Paulo will probably
have 26 million people and be the world's
second largest city. Many people arrive
with nothing. They build a one-room home
from any materials they can find
—corrugated iron, cardboard, wood —even
old clothes. Only the worst land is
available to build on. There is no water, no
drains, no roads —but São Paulo will do
because it is the city with factories and the
chance of a job. The city provides the
hope of a better life for millions of people.

53

NORTH AMERICA
Political

Life expectancy
= 10 years

47 Belize
70 Cuba
50 Haiti
65 Mexico
75 USA

- ◙ Capital city
- ● Other city

One centimetre on this map is the same as 500 kilometres on the ground.

0   1   2

Religion
Almost all the people in North America are Christian.

Main languages spoken

English   Spanish

French

10 million people

Continental population is 420 million.

Population

USA 245 million

Mexico 85 m

Canada 25 m

Honduras 4 m

Nicaragua 3.5 m

Jamaica 2.5 m

Greenland 11 000

ARCTIC OCEAN

GREENLAND

USA

Arctic Circle

C A N A D A

NORTH ATLANTIC OCEAN

DR. DOMINICAN REPUBLIC
ES. EL SALVADOR

Ottawa ◙

New York ●
Washington ◙

NORTH PACIFIC OCEAN

San Francisco ●

UNITED STATES OF AMERICA

Bermuda (UK)

Los Angeles ●

Tropic of Cancer

THE BAHAMAS
◙ Nassau

Havana ◙
Port au Prince
CUBA
DR. ●
Puerto Rico (USA)
San Juan
ANTIGUA
Guadeloupe
DOMINICA

M E X I C O

HAITI
Santo Domingo
JAMAICA ●
Kingston
ST VINCENT
GRENADA
ST LUCIA
BARB
TOBAGO
TRINIDAD

Mexico City ◙

BELIZE
◙ Belmopan
Guatemala City ◙
GUATEMALA
San Salvador
HONDURAS
◙ Tegucigalpa
ES. ● NICARAGUA
COSTA RICA
San José
◙ Managua
PANAMA
Panama City ◙

Curaçao (Neth)

The life of the na[tive] people in the far n[orth] of America h[as] changed greatly [in] recent yea[rs]

The USA is known as a 'mosaic'. People from all over the world have moved to the USA.

NORTH AMERICA
Physical

The climate of North America ranges from the freezing cold of the Arctic to the sub-tropical heat of Central America.

Coniferous forests, Canada

The Grand Canyon, Colorado River

The Bahamas

Map labels

Mt McKinley
Yukon
Mackenzie
Oodaq
Greenland
Great Bear Lake
Arctic Circle
Great Slave Lake
NORTH PACIFIC OCEAN
Hudson Bay
Rocky Mountains
Missouri
Lake Winnipeg
L. Superior
Great Lakes
Newfoundland
Great Salt Lake
California
St Lawrence
Death Valley
Colorado
Great Plains
Appalachian Mts
Rio Grande
Mississippi
NORTH ATLANTIC OCEAN
Sierra Madre
Gulf of Mexico
Tropic of Cancer
Caribbean Sea
L. Nicaragua

Legend
- Mountains
- Highlands
- Lowlands
- Deserts
- Ice cap

Fact file

Coldest place	Eismitte (Greenland) -64.8 °C (-85 °F)
Hottest place	Death Valley (USA) 48.9 °C (120 °F)
Wettest place	Guadeloupe (Caribbean) 355.6 cm per year (140.4 in)
Highest mountain	Mt McKinley (USA) 6 194 m (20 320 ft)
Longest coastline	Canada 90 908 km (56 453 miles)
Longest river	Mississippi/Missouri (USA) 6 019 km (3 740 miles)
Largest lake	Lake Superior (USA) 83 270 sq. km (32 140 sq. miles)

Interesting facts:

The longest border in the world separates the USA and Canada. It is 6 416 km (3 987 miles) long.
The world's largest trees are the Giant Sequoia in California.
The nearest island to the north pole is Oodaq, Greenland which is 706.4 km (438.9 miles) away.

NORTH AMERICA
Global Issues

Water for life
Clean water is vitally important if people are to stay healthy. Diseases carried in water kill millions of people around the world every year.

Piped water

Homes with piped water
- Over 80%
- 20%-80%
- Under 20%

Cities like Las Vegas have been built in dry parts of North America. Water for such cities has to be brought hundreds of kilometres.

Farmers require large quantities of water in order to grow crops such as grapes and cotton. This water is often taken from rivers.

The danger is that as cities grow the demand for water increase and it may be impossible to provide for the needs of the people. How can the use of water be reduced?

Las Vegas
Lake Mead
Lake Mohave
Grand Canyon
Lake Powell
Colorado River
Los Angeles
San Bernardino
San Diego
Tijuana
Salton Sea
Lake Havasu
Flagstaff
PACIFIC OCEAN
Phoenix
Tucson
Gulf of California
MEXICO
UNITED STATES OF AMERICA

Water out (canals, cities, irrigation schemes, etc)
Dam
Irrigated area
Town

Daily splash
Water is precious. Providing people with clean water costs money. The water has to be collected, cleaned and piped to where people live. There are very large differences in the amounts of water used by people in countries around the world.
More water per person is used in North America than anywhere else.

Afghanistan
60 litres
(13 gallons)

Thailand
80 litres
(17 gallons)

Mexico
130 litres
(28 gallons)

UK
175 litres
(39 gallons)

Russia
210 litres
(46 gallons)

USA
630 litres
(140 gallons)

Water consumption per person per day

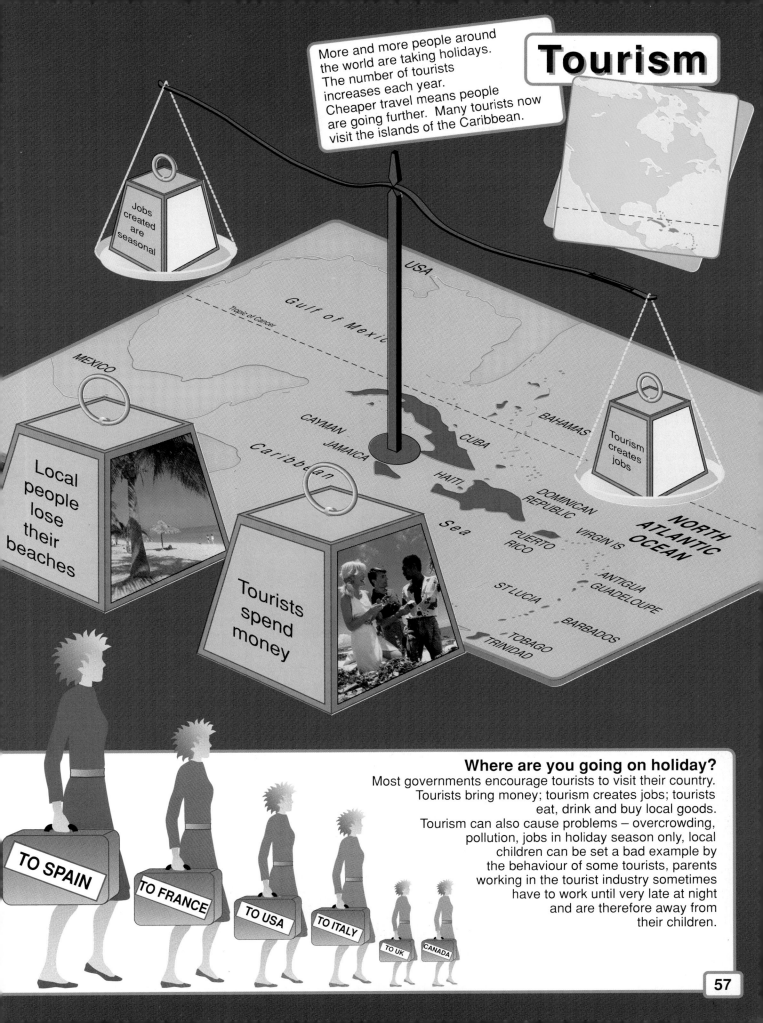

Tourism

More and more people around the world are taking holidays. The number of tourists increases each year. Cheaper travel means people are going further. Many tourists now visit the islands of the Caribbean.

Jobs created are seasonal

Tourism creates jobs

Local people lose their beaches

Tourists spend money

USA

Gulf of Mexico

Tropic of Cancer

MEXICO

CAYMAN

JAMAICA

Caribbean

HAITI

CUBA

BAHAMAS

DOMINICAN REPUBLIC

PUERTO RICO

VIRGIN IS

Sea

ST LUCIA

ANTIGUA

GUADELOUPE

BARBADOS

TOBAGO

TRINIDAD

NORTH ATLANTIC OCEAN

TO SPAIN

TO FRANCE

TO USA

TO ITALY

TO UK

CANADA

Where are you going on holiday?
Most governments encourage tourists to visit their country. Tourists bring money; tourism creates jobs; tourists eat, drink and buy local goods.
Tourism can also cause problems – overcrowding, pollution, jobs in holiday season only, local children can be set a bad example by the behaviour of some tourists, parents working in the tourist industry sometimes have to work until very late at night and are therefore away from their children.

AUSTRALASIA Political

Religion
Almost all the people in Australasia are Christian.

Life expectancy

Australia	Fiji	Kiribati	New Zealand	Papua New Guinea
75	70	58	73	50

Main languages spoken
English

Maori

Capital city
One centimetre on this map is the same as 500 kilometres on the ground.

0   1   2

A S I A

PAPUA NEW GUINEA

Port Moresby

SOLOMON ISLANDS

Honiara

Tarawa   *Gilbert Islands*

KIRIBATI

Phoenix Islands

TUVALU

WESTERN SAMOA

Pago Pago
Sam... (US...

VANUATU   Pt Vila

FIJI   Suva

New Caledonia (Fr)   Nouméa

TONGA

Tropic of Capricorn

SOUTH PACIFIC OCEAN

Cloncurry

AUSTRALIA

INDIAN OCEAN

Canberra

NEW ZEALAND   Wellington

Papua New Guinea contains many tribal people who remain proud of their traditional cultures.

Most of the population... Australia and New Zeala... are descended from settle... who came fr... Brita...

Population

Australia 16.5 million

New Zealand 3.5 m

Papua New Guinea 3.5 m

Solomon Is 300 000

Tonga 95 000

New Caledonia 60 000

Tuvalu 8 000

10 million people

Continental population is 26 million.

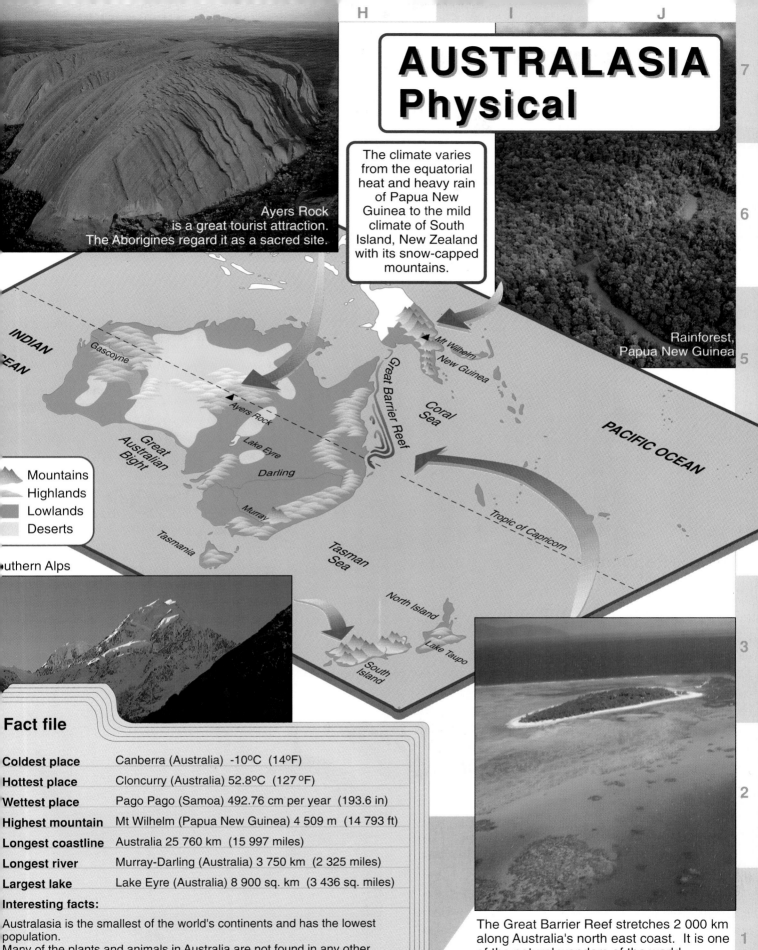

Ayers Rock is a great tourist attraction. The Aborigines regard it as a sacred site.

The climate varies from the equatorial heat and heavy rain of Papua New Guinea to the mild climate of South Island, New Zealand with its snow-capped mountains.

Rainforest, Papua New Guinea

INDIAN OCEAN

Gascoyne

Mt Wilhelm

New Guinea

Great Barrier Reef

Coral Sea

PACIFIC OCEAN

Ayers Rock

Lake Eyre

Great Australian Bight

Darling

Murray

Tasmania

Tasman Sea

Tropic of Capricorn

North Island

Lake Taupo

South Island

Mountains
Highlands
Lowlands
Deserts

Southern Alps

Fact file

Coldest place	Canberra (Australia) -10ºC (14ºF)
Hottest place	Cloncurry (Australia) 52.8ºC (127 ºF)
Wettest place	Pago Pago (Samoa) 492.76 cm per year (193.6 in)
Highest mountain	Mt Wilhelm (Papua New Guinea) 4 509 m (14 793 ft)
Longest coastline	Australia 25 760 km (15 997 miles)
Longest river	Murray-Darling (Australia) 3 750 km (2 325 miles)
Largest lake	Lake Eyre (Australia) 8 900 sq. km (3 436 sq. miles)

Interesting facts:

Australasia is the smallest of the world's continents and has the lowest population.
Many of the plants and animals in Australia are not found in any other continent. This is because Australia was isolated from the other continents and its wildlife developed quite separately.

The Great Barrier Reef stretches 2 000 km along Australia's north east coast. It is one of the natural wonders of the world. It consists of coral which is formed from the skeletons of tiny sea creatures.

59

ANTARCTICA

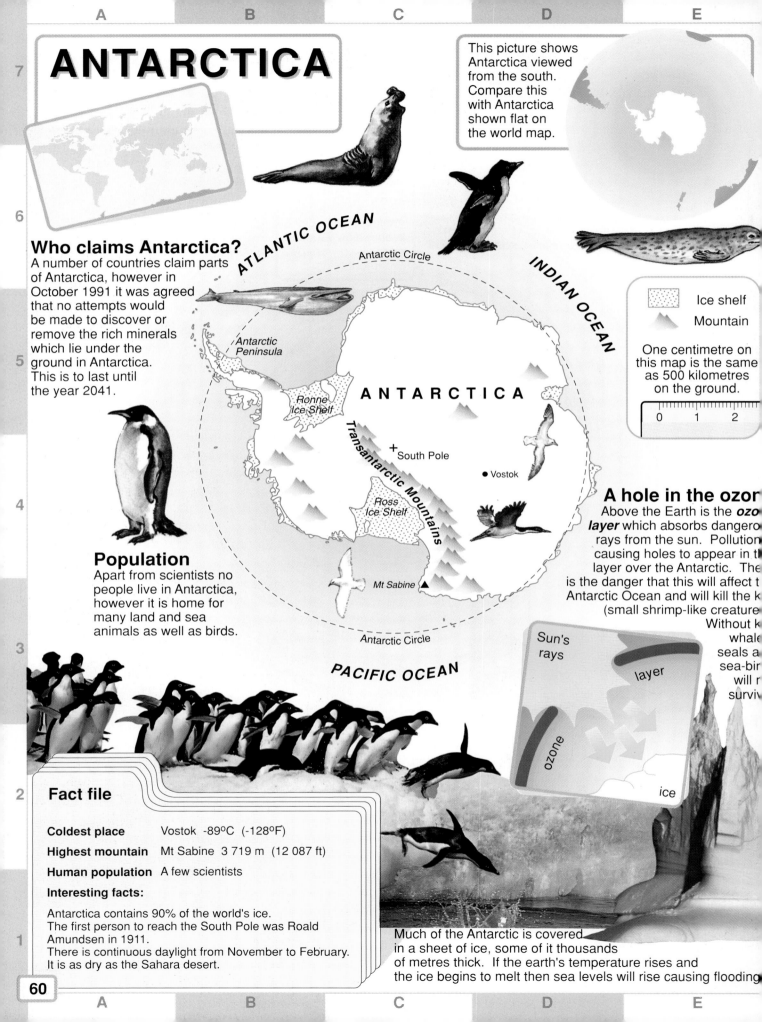

This picture shows Antarctica viewed from the south. Compare this with Antarctica shown flat on the world map.

Who claims Antarctica?

A number of countries claim parts of Antarctica, however in October 1991 it was agreed that no attempts would be made to discover or remove the rich minerals which lie under the ground in Antarctica. This is to last until the year 2041.

ATLANTIC OCEAN

INDIAN OCEAN

Antarctic Circle

Antarctic Peninsula

Ronne Ice Shelf

ANTARCTICA

Transantarctic Mountains

+ South Pole

● Vostok

Ross Ice Shelf

Mt Sabine ▲

Antarctic Circle

PACIFIC OCEAN

Ice shelf

Mountain

One centimetre on this map is the same as 500 kilometres on the ground.

0   1   2

Population

Apart from scientists no people live in Antarctica, however it is home for many land and sea animals as well as birds.

A hole in the ozon

Above the Earth is the **ozo layer** which absorbs dangero rays from the sun. Pollution causing holes to appear in t layer over the Antarctic. The is the danger that this will affect t Antarctic Ocean and will kill the k (small shrimp-like creature Without k whale seals a sea-bir will r surviv

Sun's rays

layer

ozone

ice

Fact file

Coldest place	Vostok -89ºC (-128ºF)
Highest mountain	Mt Sabine 3 719 m (12 087 ft)
Human population	A few scientists

Interesting facts:

Antarctica contains 90% of the world's ice.
The first person to reach the South Pole was Roald Amundsen in 1911.
There is continuous daylight from November to February.
It is as dry as the Sahara desert.

Much of the Antarctic is covered in a sheet of ice, some of it thousands of metres thick. If the earth's temperature rises and the ice begins to melt then sea levels will rise causing flooding

THE ARCTIC CIRCLE

Animals of the Arctic

Many animals live within the Arctic Circle on the land, on the ice and in the sea.

Many air routes cross the Arctic. If you use a globe you will see that the shortest route between many cities is across the Arctic.

- ⋰⋰ Extent of frozen ice
- — Air route

The Arctic does not consist of land. What we see on the map is not a continent but frozen ice. Submarines can sail under this ice.

Land in North America, northern Europe and Asia is inside the Arctic Circle. A variety of different peoples live there. The Inuit live there all year round. The Sami (Lapps) take their reindeer there during the summer months.

Map labels

Tokyo
Beijing
Arctic Circle
USA
Anchorage
Vancouver
CANADA
ARCTIC OCEAN
North Pole
RUSSIA
GREENLAND
Mt Gunnbjorn
Chicago
Toronto
New York
ICELAND
NORWAY
SWEDEN
FINLAND
Moscow
Helsinki
Stockholm
Warsaw
Berlin
Ankara
London
Paris
Rome
Madrid

Fact file

Highest mountain   Gunnbjorn   3 700 m   (12 139 ft)

Human population   Inuits live in the Arctic all year.

Sami live there in the summer.

Interesting facts:

During the summer the sun shines throughout the day and night, but the temperature rarely rises above 10°C (50°F).

INTERNATIONAL TIME ZONES

Wherever we live in the world when the sun rises in the east we call it morning. When it is the middle of the day in Hong Kong it is the middle of the night in New York.

We divide the world map up into 24 zones, the same as the 24 hours in the day.

When the countries of the world agreed to a common world map showing lines of longitude the start line was drawn through Greenwich in England. At that time sailors used the world map more than anyone else and the British navy was the world's largest.

The time zones sometimes bend because some countries find it convenient to keep the same time across the whole country. Other countries like the USA, Canada, Australia and Russia have a number of time zones.

Time zone legend

- Hourly zones
- Irregular zones

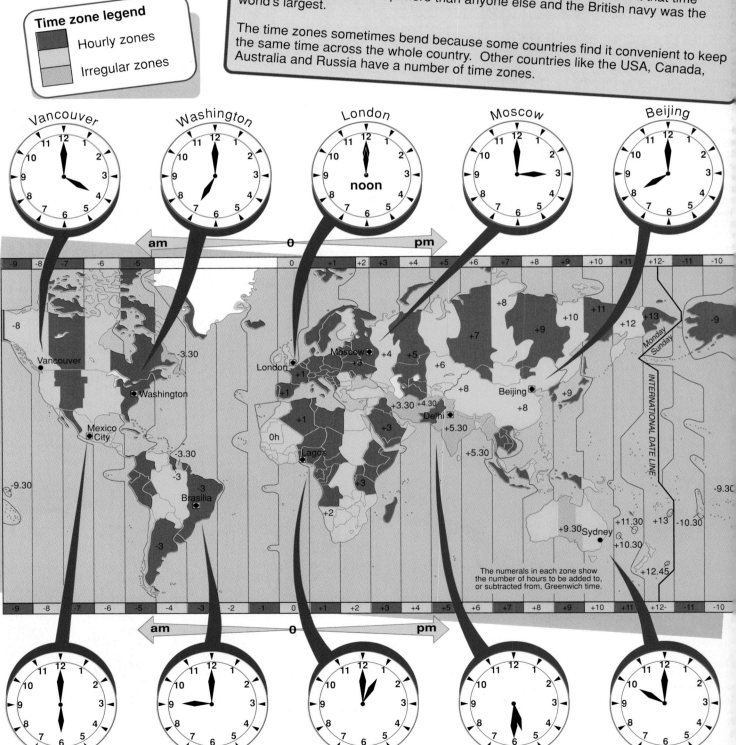

Vancouver · Washington · London · Moscow · Beijing

The numerals in each zone show the number of hours to be added to, or subtracted from, Greenwich time.

Mexico City · Brasilia · Lagos · Delhi · Sydney

63